Fresh from the Sea

Fresh from the Sea

Clodagh McKenna

GILL & MACMILLAN

Gill & Macmillan Ltd
Hume Avenue, Park West, Dublin 12
with associated companies throughout the world
www.gillmacmillan.ie

© Clodagh McKenna 2009
© Photographs by Alberto Peroli

978 07171 4657 4

Index compiled by Cover to Cover
Design by Graham Thew Design
Printed by GraphyCems, Spain

This book is typeset in 10pt on 13pt Giacomo light.

A CIP catalogue record for this book is available from the British Library.

5 4 3 2 1

Dedication

This book is dedicated to two
courageous fishermen, my Grandpop
Phil Clarke and my Uncle Pat Clarke,
who was lost at sea.

Contents

Map of Ireland's Major Fishing Ports

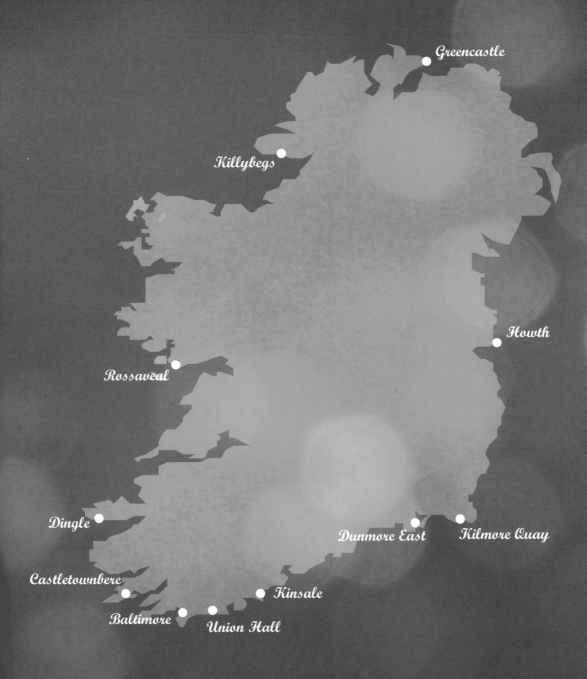

Greencastle

Killybegs

Howth

Rossaveal

Dingle

Dunmore East

Kilmore Quay

Castletownbere

Kinsale

Baltimore

Union Hall

A Guide to Fish in Season

January
Scallops, Lobster, Native Oysters, Turbot

February
Mussels, Lobster, Halibut, Native Oysters, Turbot

March
Lobster, Sardines, Native Oysters, Mussels

April
Cockles, Sea Trout, Turbot, Brown Crab, Lobster

May
Sea Trout, Sea Bass, Lemon Sole, Sardines, Brown Crab, Lobster

June
Mullet, Salmon, Herring, Lobster, Mackerel, Sea Trout, Turbot

July
Clams, Trout, Bream, Herring, Lobster, Mackerel, Turbot

August
John Dory, Crayfish, Bream, Herring, Lobster, Mackerel, Sea Trout, Turbot

September
Brown Trout, Oysters, Mussels, Bream, Brown Crab, Herring, Eel, Turbot, Mackerel, Sea Trout, Lobster

October
Oysters, Mussels, Bream, Herring, Eel, Lobster, Mackerel, Turbot

November
Bream, Herring, Lobster, Mussels, Oysters, Turbot

December
Sea Bass, Bream, Herring, Mussels, Oysters, Turbot

Acknowledgments

There are so many people who helped make this book. First, I have to thank Alberto Peroli, the photographer and a great friend; he poured every ounce of energy and creativity into this book — grazie mille! David Hare, director of the TV series *Fresh from the Sea*, who helped me get this book published — you're a gentleman and always such a pleasure to work with, and Billy Keady (cameraman) and Ray DeBrun (soundman), thank you for being so kind and patient and always making me laugh, you are fantastic to work with! To Karen McLaughlin, who has been my mentor ever since I decided to put pen to paper — thank you endlessly, you are a true friend. To everyone at Gill & Macmillan, who believed how important it was for us to turn to the sea — Sarah Liddy, Aoife O'Kelly, Kristin Jensen and Teresa Daly. To the Ferguson Family, your creativity, passion, kindness and most of all your generosity will never be forgotten, thank you for opening your home to us. To everyone at Cashelfean Holiday Homes for letting us stay in one of the most beautiful locations in Ireland, it inspired us to create this book. To Sebastiano Sardo, for being as patient with me as ever for my craziness (!) and for lending all your knowledge on wine. To my friend, business partner, and lucky for me the wife of my darling brother Jim — Erin, I don't know what I did before you came along... And to the rest of my family — thank you for under-standing this obsession I have with food! And last but most important, to all the fishermen, chefs, fishmongers and fish producers who opened their hearts and homes to me, and dedicate their lives to keeping good fish available to us all, this book is for you...

Introduction

When I started thinking about this book, I asked myself what I wanted it to achieve and I came up with five aims. I want to raise awareness about the fantastic, sustainable fish stocks we have right here, off our own shores, with plentiful supplies of mackerel, pollock, monkfish, skate, flounder, bass and even sustainable sources of tuna and arctic charr. I want to inspire you to cook fresh fish. I want to encourage people to buy fish locally, from the pier or from local fishmongers, on the day it's caught. I want us to make a real effort to protect our fish stocks and fishing grounds. Finally, I want us to get behind the people in the fishing industry – the fishermen, the fishmongers, the fish smokers – and the best way to support them is to buy their fish.

We are a nation with a history of fishing and great culinary expertise in cooking fish, yet we have turned our back on the sea as a primary food source. Let's reclaim it. It's ironic that in a time when there are so many health warnings and such concern about obesity, we are eating less fish. It is a recommended healthy source of protein, is rich in nutrients like iron, zinc and B vitamins and is also high in omega 3 essential fats. Eating fish is known to benefit the heart and the brain, to reduce depression and to help the circulatory system. So what's stopping us? Let's get cooking fish again.

I think people have bad memories of fish so overcooked it actually bounced, loaded with heavy sauce and eaten as a kind of penance. Perhaps people are also put off because they are unsure how to cook it and because the fish they buy is often of poor quality. Fish is actually remarkably simple to cook and takes no time at all. I moved to Italy three years ago and spend a lot of time travelling back to Ireland for work. When I get home to northern Italy, one of my favourite dishes to cook is pan-fried lemon sole with pistachio sauce. I love it because when I'm exhausted I need good food that's quick and uncomplicated, and this takes less than fifteen minutes to prepare and is utterly delicious. Roast fish is another quick and easy dish. On the Liguria coast near my home, they use sea bass, bream and mullet, while roast fish dishes from Ireland are more likely to use pollock, salmon or mackerel.

I have tried and tested recipes in this book that will meet a range of needs, from hearty family meals like fish pie to dinner party dishes like my squid and tomato stew, which always creates a bit of a stir but actually couldn't be easier to prepare. For this book I have also given you some of my favourite recipes from my travels to Spain, Morocco, Sicily, France, New York city and more.

Buying fresh, good-quality fish is key. I always recommend using your local fishmonger, and to that end I have included a listing on p. 197 of some of the best fishmongers and shops in Ireland. There is also a new scheme growing along the coast of Ireland whereby you can link up with the fishing boat via your mobile phone so that you get a delivery as soon as the boat comes in. The O'Driscoll brothers run a fantastic deal: a bag of fish for a fiver (€5), which is amazingly good value. You can catch them at Limerick, Kerry and Cork markets. The main thing to remember is that demand equals supply. Use your consumer power by demanding Irish-caught fish – ask the fish stallholders, the restaurant and the fishmongers where their fish was caught. If it's not Irish fish, ask them why not. If enough of us demand Irish fish, they will supply it.

I have also included an extensive store cupboard list. If you keep your store cupboard well stocked, all you have to worry about is getting fresh fish.

Some fish are better eaten in certain seasons. For example, hake and whiting are both better eaten in winter, whereas a fish like herring is better from spring to autumn. The great thing about this is that, just like vegetables, we can enjoy variety over the year and that fish bought in season is cheaper and tastes better. Perhaps even more important, fishing in this way preserves the fishing grounds (see p. xii for a list of fish in season).

The benefits of eating Irish-caught fish are twofold. First, it's fresher. Imported fish is frozen, whereas Irish fish can get from the boat to the market and onto your plate on the same day. The second benefit is that it supports the unsung heroes of the food industry – our fishermen. If you buy foreign fish, you are literally taking their jobs from them and our fishing industry will disappear. When I was making the *Fresh from the Sea* TV series on fish for RTÉ, I spent a day on a fishing boat, and let me tell you, five miles out in the Atlantic, these boys have their work cut out for them.

The fishmongers and smokers are also a big part of the industry. I visited a number of smokehouses and producers and was astounded by the quality of the products and the innovation of the producers. I have included profiles of some of the fishermen and people in the industry not just to give you a sense of how the industry works, but because they were fantastic people and I know you will enjoy meeting them as much as I did.

My big hope for the book is that it turns us back to the sea so that we think about the fish, the fishermen and also the sea itself. Just as we are becoming more ecologically aware about rainforests and ice caps, we need to think more about our oceans – about maintaining the quality of the water and not treating it as a huge dumping site for chemicals and waste. Clean water equals healthy fishing grounds and an ecologically balanced system. Fair fishing quotas and an end to the supertrawlers would help to create a sustainable fishing industry that allows the fish to breed, protects the sea bed and prevents the lamentable amount of wasted fish that the supertrawlers throw back with each catch.

The visuals in the book were created by Alberto Peroli. His photos, his knowledge of food and his eye for detail bring the recipes to life and make the producers and fishermen leap off the page. Robert Putz of Cashelfean Cottages gave me the use of his beautiful holiday home to write the book and try out the recipes. I simply could not have had a more beautiful location in which to work, situated between Durrus and Schull in West Cork, overlooking the Atlantic. I would sit down with my coffee at 7:30 a.m. to write, just as the boats set out, Atlantic bound for the day's fishing. They came back in around 4:00, just as I was packing up.

Both my grandfather and my uncles Phil and Pat Clarke were fishermen and I think every Irish person reading this book will know a fisherman in one way or another. If we want this industry to continue, it is in our hands. By supporting the fishermen, we gain fresh, locally caught, high-quality fish, in season at a reasonable price, and at its maximum nutritional value. They get to keep working and the sea benefits from a more sustainable fishing industry. We have nothing to lose – go fish this Friday and any other day you can and get your hands on a fresh catch!

Conversion Chart

These are approximate equivalents. In any recipe, use either metric or imperial measurements: never mix the two.

How to Shop for, Store and Freeze Fish

I always advise buying fish from your local fishmonger, supermarket, fish factory or farmers' market – have a look at my list of recommended outlets on p. 197. You can ask if the fish is from sustainable fishing grounds, what's best in season and for any good tips on cooking it. Find out where the fish is coming from and ask for locally caught fish. Eco-labelling is the new buzzword for sustainable, well-managed fish farms, so look out for this label when shopping for fish. Oily fish has a shorter shelf life than white fish, so keep that in mind for your menu planning when shopping.

You might notice that I haven't included cod in my recipes. This is because I feel we eat too much of it. Cod is now an endangered fish, and most of the cod that we get in Ireland is either farmed or imported, so I say let's use some of the plentiful wild fish that we have in our own waters instead.

HOW TO CHOOSE FRESH FISH

- A fresh fish should never smell fishy. It should have a very clean, clear smell, like fresh salted air.
- The eyes should be bright and clear, not cloudy and red.
- If you lift under the gills, it should be bright pink or red, not pale in colour.
- A fresh fish should be firm to the touch, not soft.
- The skin of a fresh fish should look shiny and bright, not dry and discoloured.
- The scales of the dish should be tight and moist, not dried and flaky.

CHOOSING SHELLFISH

Crabs and lobsters should be chosen by weight, as this will give you a good idea of how much meat is packed inside. Also, you want a crab or lobster that has lived a long and wild life, so the shell should reflect that with barnacles and grit. The best way to store them is submerged in water or in a box covered with an old cloth. For cooking lobsters and crabs, see p. 34. When buying mussels, make sure that all the shells are tightly closed, and if not, give them a slight tap – if they don't close, then you can't eat them. Scallops should have a firm texture; and avoid ones that look grey.

FREEZING AND DEFROSTING FISH

You can freeze fish, but a little preparation needs to go into the process.

Oily fish doesn't freeze very well because of the high oil content. The best way to freeze it is to make sure the fish is completely dry, then wrap it very well in cling film. This helps to keep out as much oxygen as possible and the fish should keep for up to three months.

White fish freezes much better and can last up to six months in a freezer. I suggest that you freeze the fish whole, not in fillets. Make sure the fish is completely dry, then wrap with either cling film or a plastic bag. Always add a label on the outside with the date and the type of fish that you are freezing.

The best way to defrost fish is by either plunging in a big bowl of cold water or placing it in the fridge and allowing it to defrost overnight. Once defrosted, make sure it's perfectly dry before cooking with it.

TIP: STORING FISH

My preferred way of storing fresh fish is wrapped in cling film, then placed on a dish of ice cubes with more cling film wrapped around the dish. This helps to keep the fish at a lower temperature than most refrigerators.

Store Cupboard for Cooking Fish

**STORE CUPBOARD FOR
COOKING FISH**

If you keep an imaginatively stocked store cupboard, it frees you up to make any number of fish-based meals in minutes, as all you have to do is pick up the fresh fish. I'm not talking a walk-in store that will keep an army marching on its stomach; I mean three shelves in a cupboard.

Keep your dry goods on one shelf: flour, rice, pasta, lentils, spices, herbs and some good stock cubes or powder. Put tinned goods e.g. tomatoes, coconut milk, chickpeas, cannellini beans, on the second shelf and your bottles and jars on the third. I recommend having three bottles of oil – a cooking olive oil, an extra virgin for dressings, and sesame. A couple of vinegars are useful (a white vinegar and balsamic) and a few sauces like soya, chilli, fish sauce and black bean are good for stir-fries. I always have jars of capers and olives on hand, as these are great with pasta and in tomato sauces. With just these few basics, you have a virtually unlimited menu at your fingertips.

I bet you can throw together a fish stir-fry faster than it takes you to queue and buy a ready-made meal. Place a fish steak on a baking tray and pop it in the oven. Chop a small onion and garlic and fry it off. Add a tin of tomatoes, a few olives and a teaspoon of capers. Pour the sauce over the roasted fish, toss a salad and in 10 minutes you have a delicious, homemade meal.

With a well-stocked store cupboard, you get all the feel-good factors of cooking, being healthy and resourceful as well as saving time and money.

PASTA:
- Farfalle
- Fusilli
- Lasagne
- Linguini
- Penne
- Spaghetti

RICE:
- Arborio
- Basmati
- Brown
- Calasparra
- Carnaroli
- Wild

SPICES:
- Bay leaves
- Black pepper
- Caraway

- Cayenne pepper
- Chilli flakes
- Coriander
- Cumin
- Curry leaves
- Curry powder
- Fennel
- Mustard seeds
- Paprika
- Saffron
- Sesame seeds
- Sunflower seeds
- Turmeric

OILS AND VINEGARS:
- Balsamic vinegar
- Extra virgin olive oil for drizzling
- Olive oil and sunflower oil for cooking
- Peanut oil
- Soya
- Tabasco
- Thai fish sauce (nam pla)
- White and red wine vinegar

NUTS:
- Almonds
- Cashews
- Hazelnuts
- Pine nuts
- Pistachios
- Walnuts

CANNED AND JARRED FOODS:
- Anchovies
- Cannellini beans
- Capers

- Chickpeas
- Coconut milk
- Dijon mustard
- Olives (black and green)
- Sardines
- Tinned tomatoes
- Tomato concentrate
- Tomato passata
- Tuna

FLOURS:
- Cornflour
- Plain
- Polenta

FRUIT:
- Lemons
- Limes

VEGETABLES:
- Aubergines
- Carrots
- Celery
- Fennel
- Onions
- Tomatoes

SALT:
- Celery salt
- Fine salt
- Sea salt
- Spicy salt

FLOUR

AGA

ROBERTS   *The Atlas of*
AMERICAN ARTISAN CHEESE   CHELSEA GREEN

Jenny Chandler   The Food of Northern Spain

The Real Food Real People Cook Book

Elizabeth David   Summer Cooking

THE EDEN COOKBOOK

Vegetables Sophie Grigson

RIVER CAFÉ COOK BOOK EAS   Rose Gray and
Ruth Rogers

THE RIVER COTTAGE MEAT BOOK
HUGH FEARNLEY-WHITTINGSTALL

Jenny Chandler
The Irish Farmers' Market

70% dark

AGA

HOMEMADE
Pies 25¢ Cakes

fresh baked fairy cakes

La Chinata

Ways of Cooking Fish

One of the beautiful things about fish is that it doesn't take long to cook. You don't have to plan ahead – you can simply buy a great-looking piece of fresh fish on the way home, throw it in a frying pan with some good old Irish butter, sprinkle on a few herbs, season and serve with salad and a chunk of bread – and it won't take you more than 10 minutes. The key thing to remember with fish is not to overcook it. It doesn't have the dense connective tissue that meat does, so it cooks much faster. The way to tell if fish is cooked is when the flesh becomes opaque.

The way you cook fish depends on the type of fish you buy. Fish loin and steaks are great for roasting in the oven on a baking tray, while a more delicate fish is better pan fried at a high heat. There are lots of fancy names for cooking fish, but basically you can fry, roast, stew, poach or grill it. Everything else is a variant, e.g. fish en papillote is essentially roasted. Look at your fish the way you would a piece of meat and let the cut, the quality and the type of fish dictate how you cook it.

POACHING

Most kinds of fish can be poached. Simply immerse the fish in simmering salted water, fish stock or milk and poach gently for 5–8 minutes, depending on the thickness of the fish. Poaching is a delicate way of cooking fish and is a particularly good way of cooking trout (see p. 136) or monkfish (see the monkfish with basil hollandaise sauce on p. 95).

STEAMING

Small whole fish or fillets steam very well. Place the fish in a steamer, cover it tightly and cook over simmering water for 10–15 minutes, depending on the thickness of the fish or the fillets. You can also add sprigs of herbs to the fish to flavour it while steaming.

GRILLING

Grilling is a fast way of cooking fish on a griddle pan or under a flamed grill. As the heat is usually high, the fish usually cooks in just 4–5 minutes, depending on the size of the fillet. When grilling whole fish, make light slashes along the skin to allow the fish to cook evenly. It's the perfect method for cooking a midweek supper.

BARBECUING

This is a great way to cook meatier fillets that have been marinated, or shellfish. The cooking time depends on the heat of the BBQ, so test as you cook. Have a look at p. 163 for tips on barbecuing and great marinades for fish.

BAKING

All kinds of fish can be baked in the oven. Fish should be covered to prevent it from drying out, either with a lid, foil or grease-proof paper. It may be baked with stuffing, on a bed of vegetables, in a pie or sauce. The time for baking a fish really depends on the size of the fish. The main difference between baking and roasting is that when baked, the fish is usually covered with sauce or potato, etc. Try my baked family fish pie on p. 89 or the baked red mullet with lemon and dill on p. 99.

Frying

PAN FRYING

This is the fastest and the easiest way of cooking fish – all you need is a frying pan. Thin fillets of fish like plaice, sole and mackerel all fry really well. Make sure your pan is hot, then add a knob of butter or some olive oil and, depending on the thickness of your fillet of fish, cook for approximately 2–4 minutes on each side (I recommend skin side down first). Try my chilli fried mackerel on p. 134 or my pan-fried sole with pistachio pesto on p. 61.

SHALLOW FRYING

The fish should be seasoned and lightly coated with flour or crumb before frying to protect it and seal in the flavour. Make sure that you use a good clean oil and a deep pan to fry it in. Once you drop the fish in the oil, use a slotted spoon to turn it when it's golden, and then once the whole fish is cooked. Drain on a plate that's lined with a paper towel. You'll love my recipe for fish and chips on p. 54, which I shallow fry.

STIR-FRYING

This is a fast and popular method of cooking, especially for Asian fish. If you can get your hands on a wok, it will allow you to reach a higher temperature and therefore cook faster. Fish should be cut into strips that are the same size as the other ingredients being used. When stir-frying, you need to use a firm-fleshed fish that won't break apart in the high heat.

GOOD FISH COOKING UTENSILS

- Filleting knife, which has a thin, bendy blade.
- Slotted spoon – for draining liquid or fat off fish.
- Fish kettle – great for poaching whole fish.
- Wok, for quickly stir-frying fish.
- Lobster pick – for reaching into those thin claws to get the meat.
- Cast iron grill – great for getting that char-grilled texture on thick fillets of fish.
- Oyster knife.
- Crab and lobster crackers – for breaking those hard shells.
- Fish prep board.

Shellfish

We tend to talk about shellfish as one whole family, when in fact it's a general term for crustacean, mollusc and cephalopod seafood. Broadly speaking, crustaceans have shells and include prawns and lobster. Molluscs can include single-shell molluscs like whelks and winkles, while bivalve molluscs are enclosed in two shells, like mussels and scallops. Cephalopods are molluscs without a shell, like squid and octopus.

When cooked, fresh shellfish is extremely healthy. Lobster and prawns are both high in vitamin B1 and B2 and mussels are high in B12. Mussels, prawns and lobsters are all high in vitamin E, calcium, iodine, potassium, selenium and zinc.

I've picked recipes using oysters, lobster, prawns, shrimp, clams, crabs, squid and mussels because all of these are widely available in Ireland. Lobsters particularly love the western coast, where there are plenty of rocks to hide under, but you will also find fabulous lobster in Waterford. They take about five years to grow and sell at just over half a kilo. They have been known to live up to fifteen years but are best eaten at about 500g–1.4kg (1lb–3lb). Males have denser, meatier flesh, while females have a more subtle flavour. I tasted the best scallops of my life when I was in Valentia, Co. Kerry – sweet, meaty and like a sugar cube melting in my mouth. For me, crab are just as delicious in flavour as lobster. The flaky meat is delicate and needs to be cooked with equally delicate ingredients, as their subtle flavour can easily be overpowered.

Mussels are a wonderful cheap, nutritious meal. Cooked in a stew of white wine and cream or a tomato sauce, they take minutes to cook and are fantastic served with a chunk of good artisan bread. When buying them, look for a smooth shell, and they should be tightly shut. The more orange mussels are female and the whiter-fleshed mussels are male. Look out for the eco standard label when you are shopping for mussels.

Prawns have become the nation's favourite shellfish and sandwich filling, but I urge you to try our own Dublin Bay prawns, which are like a smaller, slimmer lobster, and taste the difference between them and the mushy, rubbery, cooked ones so widely available now.

Fresh Oysters and Dipping Sauces

How to Open an Oyster

You will need an oyster knife, a cloth and oysters.

1 On a solid worktop place the oyster on the cloth, deep shell down and hinge towards you.
2 Cover your hand with the folded cloth and hold the oyster firmly.
3 Put the tip of the knife into the crevice at the hinge, and push it in firmly.
4 When you feel the knife has penetrated the hinge give the knife a twist to separate the shells.
5 Now change the position of the hand holding the oyster, and keeping the blade close to the top flat shell slide it in along to cut the muscle holding the two shells together.
6 Then run the knife underneath the oyster to sever the muscle from the deep shell. Then flip the oyster over in the shell but be careful not to spill any of the delicious juices.

My favourite way to eat very fresh oysters is straight down the hatch! When an oyster is really good, you want nothing to disturb that sublime experience except for maybe a glass of champagne. Saying that, a simple vinaigrette is good with fresh oysters, as well as the following sidekicks:

FOR THE VINAIGRETTE:
1 shallot, finely chopped
6 tbsps red wine vinegar
1 tbsp sugar
sea salt and freshly
   ground black pepper

SIDEKICKS
Cayenne pepper
Celery salt
Lemons
Paprika
Saffron threads
Tabasco sauce
Wasabi sauce

1 In a bowl, whisk all the ingredients together with a fork. Pour into a serving bowl and serve with a spoon.
2 Arrange oysters on a platter, preferably over ice, and place the vinaigrette in the middle.

TIP FOR A TIPPLE
Oysters glide happily along with Muscadet from Loire, champagne or a good stout.

Champagne Oysters

SERVES 2

This is a very indulgent recipe, but I think everyone deserves to indulge every now and then.

12 fresh oysters	cayenne pepper
120g butter	500ml double cream
1 shallot, finely diced	lemon slices, to serve
500ml champagne	chilled champagne, to serve
sea salt	

1 Preheat the oven to a very low temperature, e.g. 100°C.

2 Open the oysters (see instructions on p. 5) and separate from their shells, reserving the juice and the shells.

3 Place a saucepan over a low heat and add the butter. Once the butter has melted, stir in the shallot, cover and sweat for 3 minutes, or until soft.

4 Remove the lid from the pan and pour in the champagne. Leave to reduce by two-thirds.

5 Add in the juice from the oysters and season with a little salt and a pinch of cayenne pepper.

6 Poach the oysters in the liquid for 2 minutes. While the oysters are poaching, pop the oyster shells in the warm oven.

7 Remove the oysters from the liquid after 2 minutes and place back in their shells, then pop back in the oven.

8 Add the cream to the liquid and reduce by half, until you get a thick consistency.

9 Pour the cream champagne sauce over the 12 oysters and serve with a slice of lemon and, of course, a glass of chilled champagne.

Moran's Oyster Cottage *in Kilcolgan is about 10 minutes outside of Galway. This well-known pub has served Bono, Shane MacGowan, poet Seamus Heaney and even Woody Allen. Once you walk in, you'll understand why. The atmosphere is great, with a cosy bar to the front with a snug and a large room at the back. The seafood is fantastic, especially the oysters, which come directly from Michael Kelly (read more about Michael on p. 45). They also serve a wicked chowder and fresh crab on their homemade brown bread. This is definitely somewhere to spend a wet afternoon.*
Moran's Oyster Cottage, The Weir, Kilcolgan, Co. Galway. Tel: +353 (0)91 796113
www.moransoystercottage.com

Oyster Festivals

- *Don't miss the Galway International Oyster Festival, held every year on the last weekend in September. **www.galwayoysterfest.com***
- *The Clarenbridge Oyster Festival is held every year on the second weekend of September. **www.clarenbridge.com***
- *The Ballylongford Oyster Festival is held every year on the third weekend of September.*

Roasted Herb-Crusted Mussels

How to Prepare Mussels

1 The mussels should be tightly closed. If any are still open, give them a light tap on a hard surface: if they still don't close, discard them.
2 Before you cook the mussels, soak them in cold water for about 15 to 20 minutes. This allows the mussels to breathe and they will filter water and expel any sand that is inside the shell.
3 Remove any beards (thin fibres that protrude from the shell) by pulling them quickly towards the tip (hinge) of the mussel using your fingers.
4 Use a brush to brush off any barnacles, etc. that are attached to the shell.
5 Finally, remove the mussels from the water and rinse them in a fresh bowl of cold water.

SERVES 2

I see this old-fashioned recipe on menus right across Europe. It's a classic – like a good black dress, it never goes out of fashion and never lets you down. The butter and herbs gently coating the mussels make a little velvet cushion that melts once it reaches your mouth.

16 mussels, scrubbed and beards removed
100ml white wine
80g butter, softened
2 tbsp chopped thyme and parsley
150g breadcrumbs
sea salt and freshly ground black pepper

1 Preheat the oven to 200°C.
2 Place the mussels in a large pan with the white wine, cover and cook over a high heat until the mussels have opened, about 5 minutes.
3 Once all the mussels have opened, drain the liquid, discard one side of the shells and arrange the mussels in their half shells on a baking tray. Make the topping while the mussels are cooling.
4 In a bowl, mix together the butter and herbs and season with salt and pepper.
5 Spoon the herb butter into all the shells and sprinkle the breadcrumbs on top.
6 Roast in the oven for 5-7 minutes, or until the breadcrumbs are golden.

VARIATIONS

Garlic and Dill-Crusted Mussels

• Mix together 2 cloves of crushed garlic with the softened butter.
• Replace the thyme and parsley with fresh dill.

Chilli and Coriander-Crusted Mussels

• Mix together 1 finely chopped red chilli and the juice of half a lime with the softened butter.
• Replace the thyme and parsley with fresh coriander.

Lemon and Fennel-Crusted Mussels

• Mix the juice of half a lemon with the softened butter.
• Replace the thyme and parsley with fresh fennel.

Pine Nut and Basil-Crusted Mussels

• Lightly toast 100g pine nuts (or hazelnuts) in a pan, chop finely and mix in with the softened butter.
• Replace the thyme with fresh basil.

TIP FOR A TIPPLE
A Verdicchio is especially good with tomato or spicy mussels, while a Chardonnay or Chablis is perfect with creamy or steamed mussels.

While filming Fresh from the Sea, *we visited* **O'Connor's Seafood Restaurant** *in Bantry, Co. Cork, which is run and owned by Anne and Peter O'Brien. All the fish served in their restaurant is sourced locally from Bantry Bay. Anne cooked me one of their signature dishes, Mussels in Murphy's Stout (steamed in stout and cream) using the renowned Bantry Bay mussel. Heaven on a plate, especially when accompanied by a well-balanced, well-heeled 2003 Monbazillac. If you do come to O'Connor's (and you must!), make sure you order the mussels.*
O'Connor's Seafood Restaurant, The Square, Bantry, Co. Cork. Tel: +353 (0)27 50221
E-mail: oconnorseafood@eircom.net
www.oconnorseafood.com

Mussels Steamed in White Wine and Thyme

SERVES 2

My greatest memory of eating mussels goes back to when I was a child and we would holiday in Lahinch, Co. Clare. My dad is a huge lover of mussels and he would bring back a sack of fresh, locally foraged mussels to our holiday cottage and steam them just like this recipe. We would be eating them out of the pot before they were even served up!

olive oil
1 garlic clove, crushed
1kg mussels, scrubbed and beards removed (see p. 9)
100ml white wine
1 tbsp fresh thyme, finely chopped
crusty bread, to serve

1 Place a large pan over a medium heat and add a splash of olive oil, followed by the crushed garlic, and cook for 1 minute.
2 Turn the heat up to high and stir in the mussels, wine and thyme.
3 Cover and cook for 4–5 minutes. By then, the shells should have opened, which means they are cooked.
4 Remove to a large dish and serve with chunks of crusty bread to soak up the juices.

VARIATIONS

Moules Marinière
• Add 50ml fresh single cream with the white wine.
• Replace the thyme with finely chopped parsley.
• Serve with homemade French fries.

Mussels with Tomatoes and Basil
• Add 100g of good-quality Italian tinned tomatoes with the white wine.
• Replace the thyme with torn fresh basil.

Creamy Saffron Mussels
• Replace the thyme with 1/2 tsp ground saffron and 1/2 tsp ground turmeric.
• Add 100ml double cream with the white wine.

Thai-style Mussels
• Replace the white wine with 200ml coconut milk, the juice of 1 lime and 1 tbsp Thai fish sauce (nam pla).
• Replace the thyme with fresh coriander and 1 finely chopped red tiger chilli.

Spaghetti with Clams

How to Prepare Clams

These are the easiest shellfish to prepare. All you need to do is soak them in water for 10–15 minutes to allow the clams to breathe and they will filter water and expel any sand that is inside the shell.

SERVES 4

The first time I ate this dish was when I spent Christmas in Rome in 2005. It's a fabulous recipe to cook for family or friends. The juices from the clams penetrate into the pasta – it's lip-smacking good!

> olive oil
> 2 cloves garlic, crushed
> 1 onion, finely chopped
> 200g good-quality tinned chopped tomatoes
> 1 tsp dried oregano
> sea salt and freshly ground black pepper
> 100ml white wine
> 800g fresh clams, cleaned
> 600g spaghetti

1 Place a heavy-bottomed saucepan over a medium heat and add a dollop of olive oil. Lower the heat and add the garlic and onion and continue to cook until the onions are soft, about 5 minutes.

2 Add the chopped tomatoes and oregano, season with salt and pepper, stir and leave to simmer for 5 minutes. Pour in the white wine and leave for a further 2 minutes.

3 Turn up the heat to medium. Tip in the fresh cleaned clams, cover the pan and cook for about 8–10 minutes, until they have all opened, tossing them in the tomatoes every couple of minutes.

4 Cook the spaghetti in a big saucepan of boiling salted water, then drain and return to the pan.

5 Once the clams have all opened, pour into the saucepan with the drained spaghetti and toss. Serve straight away.

VARIATIONS

Mussels and Basil Linguini

- Replace the clams with mussels.
- Replace the oregano with fresh basil.
- Use linguini pasta instead of spaghetti.

Creamy Clam Spaghetti with Almonds

- Replace the tomatoes with 100ml cream.
- Omit the oregano and use 1 tsp fresh coriander.
- Add 50g flaked almonds when adding the cream.

Hot Lemon Buttered Prawns on Toast

How to Shell and Devein Prawns and Shrimps

1   To shell prawns and shrimps, first remove the head by taking a firm grip on the body and gently pulling the head away. Then hold on to the tail and remove the shell from around the body. Finally, gently tug the tail from the shrimp.

2   To devein prawns and shrimps, make a slit along the arch of the back with a small sharp knife. Rinse under cold water and remove the black vein.

SERVES 2

I love this recipe for many reasons. It's fabulous for a quick and easy starter when you have people around, but also when you have come in the door from work, tired and hungry, when you can make this in just 10 minutes.

100g butter, for frying and for toast
12 raw king prawns, shelled
juice of 1 lemon
freshly ground black pepper
4 slices good-quality bread

1   Place a frying pan over a high heat and add a big knob of butter. When the butter has melted, add the prawns and lemon juice with a good crack of black pepper.

2   Toast the bread, butter it and pile the prawns on top (3 prawns per slice).

3   Drizzle all the pan juices over the toast slices and enjoy. Heaven!

VARIATIONS

Chilli and Lime Prawns

• Finely chop 1 small red chilli and add to the melted butter.

• Replace the lemon juice with lime juice.

TIP FOR A TIPPLE
Sauvignon Blanc from Sancerre goes very well with prawns.

Fresh Shrimps in a Creamy Mustard Mayonnaise

To cook the shrimps, *simply pop them into a saucepan of boiling salted water and leave to cook for 4 minutes. They will change colour from a dark grey to pink once they have cooked. Make sure you don't overcook them, as they will become mushy inside their delicate shells.*

FOR THE HOMEMADE MAYONNAISE (makes approx. 200ml):
3 egg yolks
1 tsp Dijon mustard
pinch salt
1 tbsp white wine vinegar
100ml vegetable oil
100ml extra virgin olive oil

1 In a bowl, crack in 3 egg yolks, followed by the Dijon mustard, a pinch of salt and the white wine vinegar.
2 Measure out 100ml of vegetable oil and 100ml of extra virgin olive oil and slowly whisk into the egg yolks. The mayonnaise will begin to thicken very fast.
3 You could also add a few threads of saffron.

Prawn Risotto

SERVES 4

Ever since I moved to Italy in 2006, I have had an ongoing love affair with risotto. It takes time to make (about 40 minutes), but it's a relaxing dish to prepare. The most important thing about making a risotto is that you use a good stock and that you add it in slowly, making sure that each ladle of stock is absorbed before you add the next. The quality of the rice is also important – the best variety of rice is carnaroli, the second best is baldo and then there's the most common, arborio.

500g fresh unshelled prawns
70g unsalted butter
2 shallots or a small onion,
    finely diced
1 garlic clove, finely chopped
400g risotto rice (arborio or
    carnaroli)
sea salt and freshly ground
    black pepper
150ml dry white wine

stock (see recipe below)
1 tbsp chopped fresh flat leaf
    parsley

FOR THE STOCK:
1 carrot, sliced
1 onion or celery stalk, sliced
1 tomato, halved
1 bulb fennel, quartered
1 bay leaf

1 Cook the prawns in a large pot of salted water for 3–5 minutes, depending on their size. Drain the prawns and shell them by twisting the head to remove it and pulling the legs off. Hold the tail and then lift the shell upwards and away from the body. Don't throw out the shells; instead, make a delicious stock by placing the shells back in the water with a sliced carrot, onion or celery stalk, halved tomato, quartered fennel bulb and a bay leaf. Bring to the boil and allow to simmer for 20 minutes, then strain through a sieve.

2 Make the risotto by melting the butter in a large pan. Add the onion and garlic and cook gently for 3–4 minutes, until softened. Add the rice, season with salt and pepper and stir for a minute or so to coat it in the butter. Pour in the white wine and let it bubble for a few minutes to allow the alcohol to evaporate. Add the hot stock a ladleful at a time, stirring well between each addition until the liquid has been absorbed. This will take about 20 minutes in total.

3 Stir in the cooked prawns and allow to warm through. Just before serving, gently fold in the chopped fresh flat leaf parsley.

VARIATIONS

Scallop and Saffron Risotto

- Omit the prawns and instead pan-fry 6 scallops in butter for 2 minutes on each side, slice and fold into the risotto 2 minutes before you take the risotto off the heat.
- Replace the parsley with a few strands of saffron.

Clam or Mussel Risotto

- Replace the prawns with mussels or clams.
- Replace the parsley with dill.

King Sitric's Dublin Bay Prawns in Garlic Butter

SERVES 2

This recipe was given to me by Aidan MacManus when we went to film the TV series Fresh from the Sea. *Aidan and his wife Joan run and own King Sitric, which is a fabulous Old World restaurant with classic dishes on the menu. The view from the restaurant is directly out over Howth Harbour, where the fish is caught for the restaurant. It's a fish culinary destination and you can also stay overnight in their rooms upstairs. www.kingsitric.ie*

1 garlic clove, crushed
100ml olive oil
340g peeled prawns
splash of dry white wine
dash of Tabasco
squeeze of lemon juice
50g butter
1 tbsp fresh parsley, chopped
sea salt and freshly ground black pepper

1 Place half of the crushed garlic in a bowl with 50ml olive oil and brush over the prawns.

2 Heat another 50ml of olive oil over a low heat until smoking. Add the prawns and cook slowly.

3 In a separate pan, add the wine, Tabasco and lemon juice. Reduce by half, then add the butter.

4 Once the butter has melted, add in the prawns, the remaining garlic and the parsley. Cook for a further minute, season to taste and serve.

Potted Shrimp

Good Old-fashioned Potted Shrimps

SERVES 2

500g butter
500g shrimps
1 tsp cayenne pepper
sea salt
homemade bread, to serve

1. First, make clarified butter by gently melting 500g butter in a saucepan. Once the butter has melted, let it sit for a bit to separate. Skim off the foam that rises to the top and gently pour the butter off the milk solids, which will have settled to the bottom.

2. Cook the shrimps by placing them in a large saucepan of salted boiling water. Reduce the heat, cover the pan and simmer the shrimps for 3–5 minutes, depending on their size. The shrimps will turn pink once cooked. Drain.

3. To shell the shrimps, twist the head to remove it and pull the legs off. Hold the tail, then lift the shell upwards and away from the body. Place all the shelled shrimps in a clean Kilner jar. In a bowl, stir the cayenne into the clarified butter and pour over the shrimps, making sure the shrimps are completely covered with the butter. Leave to set in the fridge for about 1 hour. Serve with homemade bread.

TIP FOR A TIPPLE
A shrimp dish is not complete without a glass of Malvasia from Istria (Croatia), or Friuli.

Indian Shrimp Curry

SERVES 4

This is a fantastic dish to cook when you're throwing a party. You can make the recipe the day before, but leave out the shrimps. Then, when you are reheating the curry, add in the shrimps and cook for 5 minutes.

2 red chillies
vegetable oil
10 fresh curry leaves (optional)
3 garlic cloves, crushed
1 tbsp fresh ginger, finely chopped
1 tsp whole mustard seeds
1 tsp ground coriander
1 tsp ground cumin
1 tsp ground turmeric
1 onion, diced
400g tomatoes, chopped
200ml coconut milk
1kg shrimps, peeled and de-veined (see p. 16)
sea salt and freshly ground black pepper
basmati rice, to serve

1 Slice the chillies and remove the seeds if you want less heat.
2 Place a deep frying pan or casserole dish over a medium heat and add a good dollop of oil. Add in the chillies, curry leaves, garlic and ginger and cook for 2 minutes.
3 Stir in the remaining spices and continue to cook for a further 1 minute.
4 Add the onion and cook for 4 minutes.
5 Add the tomatoes and coconut milk. Cook until the tomatoes are softened, about 3–4 minutes.
6 Add the shrimps and leave to cook for 5 minutes. Season with salt and pepper.
7 Serve with basmati rice.

TIP FOR A TIPPLE
I love a Blanche beer from Belgium with a spicy fish curry.

How to Open a Scallop

1 Place the scallop on a flat board with the flat shell up. Insert the point of a strong knife between the shells and run it across the underside of the top shell to sever the internal muscle.

2 Pull the shells apart.

3 Slide the knife under the scallop to free it.

4 Lift the scallop and pull off its skirt and gut, leaving the white scallop flesh with coral attached. Remove any dark membrane.

5 Wash and dry the bottom shell to use for cooking and serving scallops.

Pan-Seared Scallops with Smoked Streaky Bacon

SERVES 2

I came up with this recipe when we were shooting the book in West Cork. I had a pack of Gubbeen smoked streaky rashers in the fridge and experimented with wrapping one of the scallops in them. The house fought over who would get to finish the dish!

4 scallops for a starter or 8 for a main course
4 (or 8) slices of smoked streaky bacon or pancetta
sea salt and freshly ground pepper
50g butter

1 Wrap the bacon around each scallop and season with salt and pepper.

2 Place a frying pan over a medium heat and add the knob of butter. Once melted, place the bacon-wrapped scallops in the frying pan. Leave to cook for 2 minutes, then turn over and allow to cook for a further 2 minutes. Eat!

Roasted Scallops in Wine and Tomatoes

SERVES 2

While we were filming the TV series Fresh from the Sea, *we headed to QC's in Caherciveen, Co. Kerry to film owner and chef Kate Cooke cooking me something delicious! QC's is a fabulous tapas-style bar and seafood restaurant. The crew, David Hare, the producer, Billy Keady, the cameraman, Ray DeBrun, the soundman, and myself perched on stools along the beautiful Irish oak bar and feasted on tapas and delicious Spanish wine. Unsurprisingly, the dishes are very Spanish influenced: local crab claws in garlic, sizzling prawns and my favourite, a dish Kate prepared for me. Here is my version of the recipe.*

> **2 scallops**
> **100ml white wine**
> **1 garlic clove, crushed**
> **2 tomatoes, chopped, or 2 tbsp tinned chopped tomatoes**

1 Preheat the oven to 200°C.

2 Prep the scallops (see instructions on p. 27).

3 Place the scallops back in the bottom part of the shells along with the white wine, half of the clove of crushed garlic and 1 tablespoon of chopped tomatoes over each scallop. Place each shell over a hot gas ring for a couple of minutes (this acts like a mini roasting dish) or alternatively leave in the oven for an extra 2 minutes.

4 When hot, transfer to the oven for 5 minutes.

TIP FOR A TIPPLE
Lagrein from Alto Adige is a light red wine that is particularly good with scallops.

How To Prepare Squid

1 Wash the squid. Remove the skin, working upwards towards the head.

2 Hold the body and tentacles and carefully pull them apart.

3 Remove head and innards from the body pouch. Avoid damaging the ink sac.

4 With a sharp knife, cut the tentacles off the head.

5 Keep the silver ink sac for other dishes (see below).

6 Pull the pen out of the body.

TIP: Uses for Black Ink

- Fantastic for adding to pasta dough for black pasta.
- Great folded through risotto.
- Add with some stock to make a black fish soup.

Mama Peroli's Squid Stew

SERVES 4 AS A STARTER, OR 2 AS A MAIN COURSE

This recipe was given to me by the photographer for this book, Alberto Peroli. It's his mama's recipe for squid. She has a wonderful gentle way with everything and this dish is just like her – gentle and uncomplicated but powerfully good!

750g squid
3 tbsp olive oil
1 onion, chopped
1 garlic clove, finely chopped
400g tin of chopped tomatoes
200ml white wine
100ml water
10 black olives, de-stoned and chopped
1 tsp dried oregano
sea salt and freshly ground black pepper

1 Clean the squid (see above) and cut the pouches into rings.

2 Heat the oil in a large, heavy-based pan over a medium heat. Add the squid and cook over a high heat, stirring from time to time, until lightly browned. Add the onion and garlic to the pan and cook for about 5 minutes, until softened.

3 Stir in the tomatoes, white wine, water, olives and dried oregano and bring to the boil. Cover and simmer very gently for 30 minutes. Season with salt and pepper.

TIP FOR A TIPPLE

Spicy fried squid is a perfect partner to a Riesling from Alsace.

Fried Squid (Calamari)

SERVES 2

I first had this dish about 10 years ago at a tapas bar in the La Boqueria market in Barcelona. It's so delicious you just keep on eating and eating it.

400g squid tubes
plain white flour, to coat
sea salt and freshly ground black pepper to taste
olive oil, for frying

1. Open up the squid tubes and slice into 2cm strips.
2. Fill a bowl with the flour and season with salt and pepper. Coat the squid in the flour.
3. Fill a frying pan two-thirds full with olive oil and place over a high heat. Once the oil is hot, dip the flour-coated squid into the oil, turning until golden brown. Drain on paper towels.
4. Serve with lemon mayonnaise (see p. 170) or a spicy tomato sauce (see below).

- For lemon mayonnaise, mix 4 tbsp mayonnaise and the juice of half a lemon together.
- For a spicy tomato sauce, place 100g of good-quality tinned tomatoes into a saucepan with a dollop of olive oil and 1 tsp paprika and season with salt and pepper. Cook over a low heat for 10 minutes.

VARIATIONS

Cajun Spiced Calamari
- Add 1 tsp Cajun seasoning and 1 tsp finely chopped coriander to the flour.

Peppered Calamari
- Add 1 tbsp freshly ground black pepper to the flour.

Chilli Calamari
- Add 1 tbsp dried chilli flakes to the flour.

Cooking Lobster and Crab

When we were making this book in West Cork, we visited my dear friend Giana Ferguson (renowned Gubbeen cheese maker) in Schull to spend an afternoon cooking lobsters and crabs. Her fabulous husband, Tom, knew a great fisherman, Jamesey from Crew Bay who could bring us fresh crabs and lobsters caught locally that morning. I always feel that cooking with friends creates better recipes, because ideas are shared and the pleasure of being in good company helps you to cook better because you are more relaxed. Herbs were picked from the garden, eggs gathered from Giana's hens and copper pots began to simmer over the Aga, which created the most delicious crab and lobster recipes. Slow food, slow cooking and slowly devoured around a table with good friends is my idea of a perfect day.

How to Cook a Live Lobster

1 To prepare the lobsters humanely, wrap them in a plastic bag and place in a deep freeze at -10–15°C for 2 hours. Then pop the lobster into a large pot of water, cover and place a weight on top of the lid. The lobster will die within 15 seconds.

2 Leave the lobster to cook for 2 minutes, then strain off the water.

3 Using a large knife, split the lobster in half lengthways, starting from the top of the tail.

4 Crack the claws and remove all the meat.

5 Remove the gravel pouch (in the head) and the intestines.

How to Cook a Live Crab

1 Bring a large pot of water to the boil and place a stalk of celery, a couple of sprigs of parsley and a couple of bay leaves in the water.

2 When the water is boiling, tip in the crab and cover with a lid. Leave to cook for 20 minutes.

3 Drain the crab from the hot water and rinse under cold water.

4 Once cooled, remove the claws and legs.

5 Turn the shell on its back and pull the body out from the tail, upwards.

6 The pale gills (known as dead man's fingers) should be discarded, as well as the stomach sac.

7 Carefully pick out the brown meat within the shell of the body.

8 Crack the legs and claws open and pull out all the white meat.

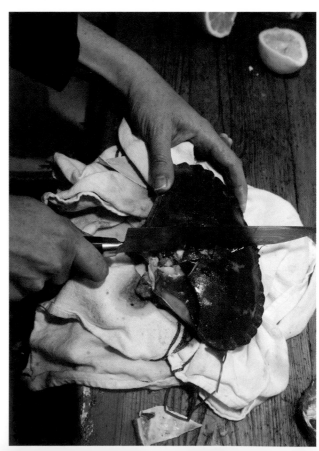

Simple Hot Buttered Tarragon Lobster

SERVES 4

2 live lobsters (700–800g total weight)
2 lemons
sea salt and freshly ground pepper
100g butter
2 tbsp fresh tarragon, finely chopped
lemon wedges, to serve

1 Follow the instructions for cooking a live lobster on p. 34.

2 Remove all the meat from the lobster and place in a bowl.

3. Mix in the juice of 2 lemons and season with sea salt and freshly ground pepper.

4 Place a large frying pan over a high heat and melt the butter. When the butter begins to foam, tip in the lobster meat. Keep flipping the pan and allow to cook for 5 minutes.

5 Just before you take the lobster off the heat, stir in the fresh tarragon.

6 Arrange the lobster tails on 4 plates and tip the lobster meat into the shells. Serve with a wedge of lemon.

Tips for Handling Crabs and Lobsters

- When you have them in a box/bucket before you cook them, place a blanket or an old cloth over them, as the darkness lulls them to sleep.
- Catch the crab from the tail end when handling to avoid any fingers getting snapped!
- Lightly stroke the lobster in between his eyes; this sends the lobster to sleep.

TIP FOR A TIPPLE
Lobster needs a bit of bubbles! A sparkling white such as champagne, Cava or Prosecco.

Lobster Newberg

SERVES 4

2 live lobsters (700–800g total weight)
3 tbsp olive oil
225ml white wine
700ml double cream
110ml sherry
pinch grated nutmeg
pinch cayenne
salt and fresh ground black pepper
10g butter
1 tbsp plain flour
50ml single cream
2 free-range egg yolks, beaten
green beans, to serve
steamed rice, to serve

1   Follow the cooking instructions on p. 34.

2   Cut the lobsters in half lengthways and remove the claws. Heat the olive oil in a large saucepan, add the claws and fry until cooked through, about 5–7 minutes. Remove and set aside.

3   Pour in the white wine and cook briskly, scraping the base of the pan to remove the lobster juices and meat. Cook until reduced by half.

4   Add the double cream and sherry and season with the nutmeg, cayenne, salt and freshly ground black pepper.

5   Add the lobster body to the pan and cook for 8 minutes. Take out the lobster and remove the meat from the shell, discarding the intestinal tract that runs down the centre of the meat.

6   In a heavy-based saucepan, melt the butter and whisk in the flour until smooth.

7   Beat together the single cream and egg yolks over a medium heat and add gradually to the flour and butter mixture, stirring until thickened.

8   Pour the cream mixture into the lobster sauce and simmer for 15 minutes.

9   Return the lobster meat and claws to the pan to warm through.

10 To serve, place the lobster pieces on a plate and pour over the creamy sauce. Serve with steamed rice and lightly blanched green beans.

Crab Cakes with Lime Guacamole

MAKES 4 CAKES

2 slices of good-quality bread, made into rough breadcrumbs
400g white crabmeat
2 tbsp homemade mayonnaise (see p. 170)
a drop of Worcestershire sauce
1 egg, beaten
1 dstsp fresh tarragon, finely chopped
juice of 1 lemon
sea salt and freshly ground black pepper
50g butter

1   Place all the all the ingredients except the butter in a bowl and season lightly with salt and pepper. Mix well.

2   Form the crab mixture into round patties.

3   Place a frying or griddle pan over a medium heat and add the butter.

4   Once the butter begins to foam, add the crab cakes and cook for 3 minutes. Turn over and cook for a further 2 minutes. They should be golden in colour.

5   Serve with lime guacamole.

LIME GUACAMOLE

1 very ripe avocado
1 garlic clove, crushed
2 tbsp freshly squeezed lime juice
1 tbsp extra virgin olive oil
1 tbsp chopped fresh coriander
sea salt and freshly ground black pepper

1   Cut the avocado in half, remove the stone and scoop out the flesh.

2   Mash with a fork, then add the garlic, lime (or lemon) juice, olive oil and coriander and mash together well. Season to taste with salt and pepper. Cover with cling film immediately, as it discolours very quickly.

Tip: To keep your guacamole nice and green, place the avocado stone on top of the dip and cover with cling film.

Crab Salad

SERVES 4 AS A STARTER

2 fresh crabs
3 tbsp homemade mayonnaise (see p. 170)
1 scallion, finely chopped
4 very ripe cherry tomatoes, halved
juice of $^1/_2$ lemon
1 sprig flat leaf parsley, chopped
sea salt and freshly ground black pepper
homemade brown bread, to serve

1   Follow the instructions on p. 34 for cooking the crabs.

2   Place a mix of brown and white crabmeat, mayonnaise, scallion, tomatoes, lemon juice and parsley in a bowl. Season with salt and pepper and mix well.

3   Serve with homemade brown bread.

TIP FOR A TIPPLE
Pinot Grigio or a Tocai are wonderful with crab dishes.

Classic Shellfish Bisque

SERVES 4

This is a fabulous way to use up all the shells from the fish. Its flavour is rich and intense.

100g butter
1 onion, peeled and diced
2 carrots, peeled and sliced
1 celery stalk, diced
800g shells from prawns, crabs, lobster, etc.
1 sprig thyme
1 bay leaf
40ml brandy
2 tbsp tomato purée
100ml tomato passata
1 ¹/₂ litres fish stock
sea salt and freshly ground black pepper
100ml cream
1 tsp paprika
toasted baguette slices, to serve

1. Place a large saucepan or casserole dish over a medium heat and add the butter.
2. Once the butter has melted, stir in the onion, carrot and celery. Cover and allow to cook for 3 minutes.
3. While the vegetables are cooking, break up the shells into tiny pieces with a large knife. Add the shells into the vegetables along with the sprig of thyme and bay leaf. Stir well and allow to cook for 1 minute.
4. Pour the brandy into the pan and leave to evaporate. Stir in the tomato purée and passata. Leave to cook for 5 minutes.
5. Add in the fish stock. Season with salt and pepper and simmer for 30 minutes.
6. Stir in the cream and paprika. Taste the bisque and once it has reached a delicious flavour, pass it through a sieve. Serve with toasted slices of baguette.

Michael Kelly

Michael Kelly, now in his eighties, has lost none of the passion and enthusiasm for the oysters he started selling over 50 years ago. As we pored over old photos and talked about his company, Kelly Oysters, his eyes sparkled with pride and excitement about how the business was then and how it is still growing and expanding now.

The Kelly family can trace their history in the area back to the 17th century. Michael grew up in a house overlooking Galway Bay. In the 1950s, when there was no work for young men in Ireland, he saw each of his siblings emigrate to England to find work. But Michael had an idea for a business and decided to stay. He believed he could sell oysters to the Irish.

He started with just one boat that his uncle gave him. Pretty soon he had two boats, then 20. He started buying oysters from the fishermen in the Clarinbridge area when the shells were three inches long and bedding them, in large rope sacks, along the Atlantic coast where the Kilcolgan River runs into the sea. When the oysters reached maturity at around five years, they were harvested and sold. By 1954, Michael was supplying Paddy Burke's, a famous local pub where Princess Margaret and Lord Snowdon indulged in a dozen oysters on more than one occasion. Soon the business was expanding enough to start exporting, but Michael refused to sell his oysters as French or Dutch oysters, as was common then. He pushed and fought for his oysters to be called Galway oysters and he won the battle. By the 1960s, Michael had become one of Ireland's main oyster suppliers, with his Galway oysters now the choice of the fashionable eating houses of the day.

In 1963, Michael married Bernadette and their family and business grew in tandem. In the 1970s they started exporting shellfish to France and Spain, and by the 1980s they had moved into the German market, supplying restaurants and hotels with Kelly's Galway oysters. Further expansions into the Swiss market saw Michael Kelly (Shellfish) Ltd become one of the leading suppliers across Europe.

Today, Kelly's Oysters is run by Michael's sons Diarmiud and Michael, Jr. Their oyster beds are still in the inner Galway Bay adjacent to Clarinbridge. This is the perfect environment for oysters, growing in grade A listed water, flushed twice a day by the Atlantic tides, filtering 11 litres of pristine water every hour – just the right mix of fresh and sea water. Kelly's Oysters is the main supplier of the Galway Oyster Festival, which gets through an average of 100,000 oysters a week. I met the family when I was there filming *Fresh from the Sea*, and in fact Michael's son was himself the oyster shucking champion in 2007.

I don't mind admitting I fell a bit in love with Michael Senior. When we went to meet him, he was beautifully dressed in a smart suit. We barrelled in, all pressed for time and eager to get the photos done, but Michael Kelly is his own man. He is not to be rushed, picking his words slowly and carefully. He showed us the old black and white photos of the oystermen back in the 1950s and 1960s, harvesting the oysters, and photos of himself with Paddy Burke. What is clear from the photos and the stories is that Michael is a traditional Irishman, a family man and a great pioneer. What is most remarkable is that after over 50 years in the business he is just as passionate about it as he was when he was a young man. It was a cold blustery day when we visited, but that didn't deter him – he insisted we all go down to the oyster beds and eat them fresh from the sea. It was one of those culinary experiences you don't forget. Many people believe that Galway oysters are the best in the world, and after my first mouthful, I am in complete agreement. Oysters can be salty or sweet, and these were sweet and meaty and totally delicious. Oysters can be eaten smoked, boiled, baked, fried, roasted, stewed, canned or pickled, but for me, the only way to taste an oyster that good is raw from the shell with a squeeze of lemon.

When we got back to the house, Bernadette, Michael's wife, had baked fresh brown bread to serve with the oysters and a glass of milk (Michael is teetotal). This is a traditional Irish way of eating them, though more often they are served with a glass of stout.

What impresses me so much about Michael is that he believed 100 per cent in the product, even when people told him he was mad. Work was scarce in Ireland in the 1950s, and to make ends meet Michael used to row five miles to deliver post to an island off the coast and five miles back. But he never gave up. He kept on believing and he kept on pushing. Starting from nothing in the 1950s, he has built an oyster empire. He has 14 grandchildren and now a third generation of the family are entering the business. It is a source of great pride to Michael that all his own children are involved in the business and none of them has emigrated or moved away.

He doesn't have to prove himself these days – his oysters are acclaimed by the world's top chefs and served in Ireland's best restaurants. The world really is his oyster.

Michael Kelly (Shellfish) Ltd
'Aisling', Tyrone, Kilcolgan, Co. Galway
Tel: +353 (0)91 796120
Fax: +353 (0)91 796720
E-mail: kellyoysters@eircom.net
www.kellyoysters.com

Flat Fish

Flat fish ain't the prettiest, with their protruding eyes that are too close together on top of their heads, but they taste gorgeous and are quick and easy to cook. The flat fish you are most likely to come across are plaice, sole, halibut, turbot, brill, dab and flounder. They are very easy to fillet as long as you have a sharp and flexible knife – I'll show you how on p. 51. And do keep the trimmed fins, head and tail for stock – see my recipe for stock on p. 53.

Fish like sole and plaice are delicate, flaky fish, so they cook quickly and are better suited to light sauces like à la meunière (browned butter with parsley and lemon). I have included a posh fish and chips recipe, plaice in a tempura batter. The lightness of the batter goes perfectly with the delicate texture and flavour of the fish. The thing to remember with flat fish is that it loses moisture quickly, so if you are roasting it, always put a little water or wine in with it. Cooking flat fish en papillote is an excellent way to retain moisture and keep the fish succulent (see my recipe for tarragon plaice on p. 63).

Turbot, the chef's favourite, and halibut are much firmer and can be cut and cooked as steaks. My favourite, though, has to be sole, pan-fried quickly in butter with lemon juice and a handful of parsley – sweet, delicate and utterly delicious (see the recipe on p. 70).

How to Fillet a Flat Fish

1 Lay the fish on a board with the head pointing away from you.

2 Cut around the head and down the centre or lateral line of the fish right through to the backbone.

3 Working on the fillet nearest to you, insert the point of the knife under the flesh at the head end. Keeping the knife blade parallel to the bones, slice away the fillet using long, sweeping strokes.

4 Remove the other fillet in the same way, but turn the fish around so that the tail is pointing away from you and cut from tail to head.

5 Repeat the whole process on the other side to obtain the remaining two fillets, giving you four quarter-cut fillets.

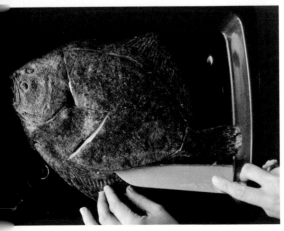

Fish Stock

MAKES APPROX. 1 LITRE

Making fresh fish stock makes a huge difference to the overall taste of fish stews and soups. It uses up all the bones that would ordinarily be thrown out. It is preferable to use white fish rather than oily varieties, which can be pungent and gelatinous.

2kg fish bones from sole or turbot
200ml white wine
2 carrots, sliced
1 stalk of celery, sliced
1 bay leaf
sprig fresh thyme
fresh bunch of flat leaf parsley
6 black peppercorns

1 Place all the ingredients in a large saucepan.

2 Cover with cold water and bring to the boil. Allow to simmer for 20 minutes, skimming off the white foam from the top of the stock.

3 Remove the stock from the stove, stir it again and allow it to steep for 10 minutes. Strain through a sieve.

4 Cover the stock after it has completely cooled and keep refrigerated for up to 3 days, or freeze for up to 2 months.

Posh Fish and Chips with Homemade Tartare Sauce

SERVES 4

A good fish and chips meal is definitely up there on the list of our nation's favourite dishes, and certainly on mine! The most important aspect of making fish and chips is that you have a chilled batter and that you use good clean oil to fry the fish in.

FOR THE PLAICE AND CHIPS:
vegetable oil
900g floury potatoes, peeled and cut into chips
olive oil
sea salt and freshly ground black pepper
8 fillets of plaice, cut into long strips

FOR THE BATTER:
500ml water
1 egg
200g plain flour

1 Preheat the oven to 180°C.
2 First, make the batter for the fish. Chill 500ml of water in a freezer, then whisk in 1 egg and 200g plain flour.
3 Half fill a deep frying pan with vegetable oil and place under a high heat.
4 While the oil is heating up, drizzle a good dollop of olive oil over the raw chips, season with salt and pepper and give them a good shake to make sure the chips are well coated.
5 Place the chips in a roasting tin and pop in the preheated oven for 25 minutes, or until they are golden and cooked all the way through.
6 Dip the plaice strips into the batter and from there straight into the hot oil. Turn after a couple of minutes (or when you get a nice golden colour on the fish). Remove all the fillets from the pan onto a plate lined with paper towels. Season with salt and pepper and serve with my delicious tartare sauce (see the recipe on p. 56).

TIP FOR A TIPPLE
Fish and chips is delicious with a Blanche Belgian beer.

TARTARE SAUCE
3 egg yolks
1 tsp Dijon mustard
sea salt
1 tbsp white wine vinegar
100ml vegetable oil
100ml extra virgin olive oil
1 tsp capers, drained
1 tsp gherkins, sliced
1 tsp parsley, chopped finely (optional)
1 tsp chives, chopped finely (optional)

1 In a bowl, crack in 3 egg yolks, followed by the mustard, a pinch of salt and the white wine vinegar.

2 Measure out 100ml of vegetable oil and 100ml of extra virgin olive oil and slowly whisk into the egg yolk mixture. The mayonnaise will begin to get thick and creamy.

3 Stir in the capers, gherkins and herbs (optional).

TIPS
- You can use any kind of fish for this recipe.
- Mix 1 tbsp of Ballymaloe Country Relish with 200ml mayonnaise for a spicy mayonnaise relish to serve with this recipe.
- To make fish fingers for kids, slice fresh fish fillets into 5cm strips, dip first in milk, then flour and lastly breadcrumbs and bake in a preheated oven at 160°C for 15 minutes.
- This is also a great recipe for a party – just double or treble the ingredients (depending on how many people are coming) and you can keep the fish and chips warm in an oven until you are ready to serve them. Try serving them in small coloured paper cups with a thin slice of lemon – they'll look fab!
- For quick mushy peas, tip frozen peas into a saucepan of boiling water for 3 minutes, drain and transfer to a food processor. Season with salt and pepper, add in a knob of butter and a drizzle of the water that you cooked the peas in. Blitz for a couple of minutes and that's it!
- To make a beer batter, place 400g flour in a bowl and season with salt and pepper. Make a well in the centre and whisk in 200ml of lager (or stout if you prefer) and 300ml chilled sparkling water. Chill the batter in the fridge for 1 hour before you use it.

I love a good fish and chips. I look for a light, crispy batter with flaky, moist (but not wet!) fish and homemade chips – this isn't easy to find! But while we were travelling around Ireland filming the Fresh from the Sea series, I found the best fish and chips that I have eaten in years at the **Oar House** *in Howth. The batter was clean, thin and crisp and the fish perfectly flaky and moist, served with a beautiful homemade tartare sauce and creamy mushy peas. So if you've got the craving, now you know where to go!*
Oar House, West Pier, Howth, Co. Dublin. Tel: +353 (0)1 839 4562 **www.oarhouse.ie**

Plaice à la Florentine

SERVES 4

The first time I was lucky enough to taste this dish was when I was about 15 years old in France. It's rich and creamy, but the spinach adds a lovely freshness to the dish.

4 fillets of plaice (approx. 180g per fillet)
40g butter
spinach, stalks removed
Mornay sauce (see p. 169)
mature cheddar cheese, grated
sea salt and freshly ground black pepper

1 Preheat the oven to 200°C.
2 Sauté the spinach with the butter. Drain and completely cover the bottom of an ovenproof serving dish with the spinach.
3 Put the plaice fillets on top of the spinach and cover with Mornay sauce (see p. 169). Follow with the grated cheese and season with salt and pepper.
4 Pop in the oven for 10–12 minutes. This is delicious served with ratatouille (see p. 179).

TIP FOR A TIPPLE
A Muscadet from Loire is great with this creamy fish dish.

Fritto Misto

SERVES 4

This is the most popular fish dish in Italy. It's served in big platters, usually with no sauce to accompany it, but I love serving it with homemade lemon mayonnaise. It's a fantastic dish to cook when you have lots of people coming round, and you can use all different types of fish in the dish – delizioso!

vegetable oil, for frying
100ml milk
200g flour, seasoned with salt and 1 tsp cayenne pepper
1kg mixed small fish (plaice, sole, whitebait, sprats, etc.)
sea salt and freshly ground black pepper
lemon wedges, to serve

1 Place a deep frying pan or saucepan over a high heat and fill about 8cm with oil.

2 Fill a bowl with the milk and another with the flour. Lay a few sheets of paper towel in a large dish for placing the fish on once it's fried.

3 Dunk the fish into the milk, then coat in the seasoned flour, shaking off any excess flour.

4 Drop the coated fish into the hot oil and cook for 3–4 minutes. Remove once golden in colour with a slotted spoon and transfer to the paper-lined plate to drain off the excess oil. Serve with a lemon mayonnaise (see p. 170).

TIP FOR A TIPPLE
Pinot bianco from Friuli in Italy.

Flat Fish   59

Lemon Sole Pan-fried in a Pistachio Pesto

SERVES 2

I made a dish similar to this when I was asked to appear on Richard Corrigan's programme Corrigan Knows Food *to try to encourage families to eat better. The family in question loved this recipe and I think you will too.*

4 fillets of lemon sole
a little oil

FOR THE PESTO:
110g fresh basil leaves
150ml extra virgin olive oil
50g pistachio nuts, shelled
1 garlic clove
50g freshly grated Parmesan
pinch of salt

1   First make the pesto by placing all the pesto ingredients in a food processor. Blend for 2 minutes.

2   Place the sole fillets in a large bowl, pour the pistachio pesto over them and baste well.

3   Place a frying pan over a medium heat, add a drop of oil and add the fillets to the pan. Cook on each side for 2 minutes. Eat straight away!

VARIATIONS

Lemon Sole Pan-fried in Basil Pesto

• Replace the pistachios with pine nuts.

Lemon Sole Pan-fried in Coriander, Hazelnut and Lemon Pesto

• Replace the basil with fresh coriander.
• Replace the pine nuts with hazelnuts.
• Add the juice of half a lemon.

TIP FOR A TIPPLE
Rancio sec from southern France is great with a pistachio pesto.

South Kerry is a haven for great fish. I ate the best shrimp and scallops on Valentia Island, and just over the bridge back on the mainland of Portmagee you'll find the wonderful **Moorings pub/restaurant/guesthouse** – *my little hidden treasure. If you go there, and you must, order the black sole – it falls off the bone and melts within seconds in your mouth. You can work it off by dancing the night away at their famed traditional dancing nights in the bar! The Moorings, Portmagee, Co. Kerry. Tel: +353 (0)66 947 7108* **www.moorings.ie**

Tarragon Plaice en Papillotes Served with a Julienne of Vegetables

SERVES 2

A classic French method of cooking fish, this keeps the texture of the fish delicate, moist and crumbly. You can use any flat fish for this recipe and it's also great served with a hollandaise or béarnaise sauce (see p. 169).

FOR THE TARRAGON PLAICE:
4 fillets of plaice
4 rectangles of greaseproof paper, each big enough to hold 1 fillet of fish
4 tbsp double cream
sea salt and freshly ground black pepper
2 tbsps fresh tarragon, chopped
juice of 1 lemon

FOR THE JULIENNE:
1 carrot, peeled
1 leek
1 courgette
50g butter
sea salt and freshly ground black pepper

gratin dauphinois, to serve (see p. 178)

1 Preheat the oven to 220°C.
2 Place 1 fillet of plaice in the middle of each sheet of greaseproof paper.
3 Pour 2 tbsp of double cream on top of each parcel and season with salt and pepper. Scatter the tarragon leaves over the fillets and pour over the lemon juice.
4 Fold the edges of the greaseproof paper together to create 4 small tent-like shapes.
5 Place in the preheated oven for 15 minutes.
6 While the fish is cooking, make the julienne of vegetables by shredding the vegetables into very thin strips.
7 Place a frying pan over a medium heat and melt the butter. Stir in the vegetables and cook for 10 minutes. Season with salt and pepper.

8 Bed the serving plates with the julienne of vegetables. Place the fish on top and pour the juices from the parcels over the fish.

9 Serve with a gratin dauphinois (see p. 178).

VARIATION

Plaice en Papillotes with Capers and Tomatoes

- Omit the cream and add 1 tsp of capers in each parcel instead.
- Omit the tarragon and add 1 small sprig of thyme.

TIP FOR A TIPPLE

Gavi from south-eastern Piedmont creates a wonderful balance with the plaice.

Fillets of Turbot with Creamy Leeks

SERVES 2

> 1 large leek
> 70g butter
> 2 large turbot fillets, approx. 100g per fillet
> sea salt and freshly ground pepper
> 50ml cream
> lemon wedges, to serve

1 Thinly slice the white of the leek. Place in a colander, rinse under water and allow to dry.

2 Place 2 frying pans over a medium heat and divide the butter between the 2 pans. Once the butter has melted, add the turbot fillets to one pan and the leeks to the other. Season with salt and pepper.

3 After 3 minutes, turn the fish over and add the cream to the leeks. Lower the heat under both pans and continue to cook for 5 minutes.

4 Once the leeks are soft and the fish is cooked, bed 2 serving plates with the leeks and place a turbot fillet on each.

5 Pour the creamy juices from the leek pan over the fillets and serve with a wedge of lemon.

TIP FOR A TIPPLE
Try an Albariño from northern Spain.

Baked Turbot with Watercress Butter

SERVES 4

This is one of the simplest ways of cooking fish, and if your fish is spanking fresh, there is no better way to cook a flat fish, in my humble opinion. You can use plaice, brill, black sole or Dover sole instead of the turbot for this recipe and the watercress can be replaced with dill, wild garlic or fennel.

1 whole turbot, approx. 2kg
water
sea salt

FOR THE WATERCRESS BUTTER:
1 bunch of fresh watercress (approx. 10 sprigs)
100g butter, softened
juice of $^1/_2$ a lemon

1   Preheat the oven to 200°C.

2   Score the flesh of both sides of the turbot quite deeply and diagonally at 5cm intervals. Season the fish well with sea salt and place the turbot, pale skin side down, in a large roasting tin. Pour in enough water so that half of the fish is immersed. Pop in the preheated oven for 30 minutes, or until the flesh of the fish is cooked (when cooked, the flesh will be white and will come away from the bone easily).

3   While the fish is cooking, make the watercress butter. Tear the leaves off the stalks and chop finely, then place in a bowl. Add the softened butter to the bowl along with the juice of half a lemon. Beat well, until all the watercress is well mixed through the butter. Tip the butter out onto a piece of cling film and shape the butter into a log about 2 $^1/_2$cm in diameter. Wrap the log in the cling film and place in the fridge to allow it to set.

4   Once the turbot is cooked, remove from the oven. Carefully remove the skin and tip the fillets onto a serving dish. Take the watercress butter out of the fridge, cut into slices and place on top of each of the fillets. Delicious served with boiled new potatoes.

TIP FOR A TIPPLE
Gavi from south-eastern Piedmont creates a wonderful balance with the plaice.

Crunchy Crusted Brill

SERVES 4

Parmesan and buttered pine nuts capping a delicious fresh piece of brill is a mouthful of heaven. You can use hazelnuts or almonds instead of the pine nuts, and a sprinkle of finely chopped semi sun-dried tomatoes on top would also be glorious.

150g grated Parmesan or Desmond cheese
80g pine nuts
4 slices of stale bread, made into crumbs
70g butter, melted
4 large fillets of brill
sea salt and freshly ground black pepper

1 Preheat the oven to 180°C.
2 Begin by making the crunchy topping. Place the Parmesan, pine nuts, bread-crumbs and melted butter in a blender or food processor and pulse for just 1 minute. You want the mixture to maintain its crunchiness, so it can't be too fine.
3 Place the fillets on a roasting tray and season each side with salt and pepper. Spoon the crunchy topping over the fillets and place in a preheated oven for 15 minutes, or less if the fillets are thin.
4 Serve with French beans or a green salad.

TIP FOR A TIPPLE
Chardonnay from New Zealand.

Sole à la Meunière

MAKES 2 LARGE PORTIONS OR 4 SMALL PORTIONS

This is probably the first way that I ever cooked fish. It's a great method of cooking for the time-starved world that we live in – 5 minutes and you have supper!

4 sole fillets
sea salt and freshly ground pepper
60g flour, seasoned with sea salt and freshly ground black pepper
80g butter
1 ¹/₂ tbsp parsley, finely chopped
juice of 1 lemon
lemon wedges, to serve

1 Season both sides of the sole with salt and pepper. Dust the fillets in the seasoned flour and shake off any excess.

2 Place half the butter in a frying pan or skillet. When the butter begins to foam, add the fillets of sole and sauté for 2 minutes on each side. Remove the fish to serving plates and keep warm.

3 Place the pan back on the heat and add the remaining butter along with the chopped parsley and lemon juice. Once the butter has melted and is a light brown colour, remove from the heat and pour over the fish. Serve with a couple of lemon wedges.

TIP FOR A TIPPLE
Penedès from Catalonia.

Black Olive Sole

SERVES 4

This is a dish that is eaten a lot in Liguria. You can also use plaice for this dish.

olive oil
1 garlic clove, sliced
1 tbsp parsley, finely chopped
70g flour, seasoned with sea salt
4 fillets of sole
juice of 1 lemon
30 black olives, pitted and sliced in half

1   Place a frying pan over a low heat and drizzle in a dollop of olive oil.

2   Add the garlic and parsley to the pan and sauté for 2 minutes.

3   In the meantime, dip the sole fillets into the seasoned flour to lightly coat them. Add the sole to the frying pan and squeeze the lemon juice over the fish (after you do this, slice the lemon into thin slices). Allow to cook for 2 minutes, then turn over.

4   Once you have turned the fish over, sprinkle over the halved olives and scatter the lemon slices on top. Leave to cook for a further 3 minutes and serve.

TIP FOR A TIPPLE
Verdicchio from Marche.

Roasted Sea Bream with Sun-dried Tomatoes, Lemon and Garlic

SERVES 2

The lemon, garlic and tomatoes ooze their flavours through the slits and right down into the meat of the fish. You can use this recipe with any whole fish and I love to serve it with my potato roasties (see p. 176)

2 lemons
1 sea bream, weighing approx. 500g, cleaned and scaled
2 garlic cloves, sliced
12 sun-dried tomatoes
sea salt and freshly ground black pepper
olive oil

potato roasties, to serve (see p. 176)

1 Preheat the oven to 180°C.

2 Slice the lemons, then cut into quarters.

3 With a sharp knife, make 9 slits on one side of the fish. Push a slice of lemon, a slice of garlic and a sun-dried tomato in each of the slits.

4 Place the fish in a roasting tin and scatter the remaining lemons, garlic and tomatoes in the tin. Sprinkle over some sea salt and freshly ground pepper, followed by a good drizzle of olive oil.

5 Pop in a preheated oven for 20 minutes. Serve with some potato roasties (see p. 176).

TIP FOR A TIPPLE
Riesling from the Mosel Valley in Germany.

Creamy Fennel, Parmesan and Turbot Gratin

SERVES 4

The aniseed-like flavour from the fennel is subtle, but it perfectly compliments the delicate flavour of the turbot. The Parmesan gives a nutty, salty finish to this wonderful dish that is so easy to prepare.

50g butter
2 fennel bulbs, thinly sliced
4 fillets of turbot
sea salt and freshly ground black pepper
200ml cream
100g Parmesan, finely grated

1   Preheat the oven to 180°C.
2   Grease an ovenproof serving dish with butter.
3   Layer the thinly sliced fennel on the bottom of the dish.
4   Lay the turbot on top of the fennel and season with salt and pepper.
5   Pour over the cream and sprinkle over the grated Parmesan cheese.
6   Bake in the preheated oven for 20 minutes. Serve with a big green salad.

TIP FOR A TIPPLE
Arneis from Roero in northern Italy.

Thomasina Miers's Mexican Red Snapper with Refried Beans

SERVES 4

I first met Thomasina Miers when I was teaching at the Ballymaloe Cookery School about seven years ago. Her energy and enthusiasm for good food were intoxicating and we immediately became friends. After she finished the course, she went on to make cheese at the Gubbeen Farmhouse in Schull. At the time, I had just moved to Schull, so when she finished her time at Gubbeen she joined me for a month in my escapades at the farmers' markets. We would make fresh pasta, focaccia, chocolate truffles – anything that sprang to mind! Our next adventure together was baking soda bread at the Salone Del Gusto (the largest food festival in the world, which is run by Slow Food). I carted over dozens and dozens of pints of buttermilk on the plane, and each morning of the festival we baked Irish soda bread at 6:00 a.m. for thousands of foreigners to eat with Irish wild smoked salmon.

Then Thomasina returned to London and enjoyed various adventures, like cooking at Villandry (a beautiful French deli and restaurant), running a restaurant in Mexico and then winning BBC's Masterchef *in 2005. She writes a column for the Body and Soul section of* The Times, *and her first book,* Cook, *was published by HarperCollins in October 2006. In her Channel 4 television series,* The Wild Gourmets, *Thomasina travelled across Great Britain, catching and cooking the land's finest wild food. Her most recent programme for Channel 4 is* A Cook's Tour of Spain. *Thomasina runs and owns the Mexican restaurant Wahaca in Covent Garden, London (www.wahaca.co.uk). I love her and her food to bits!*

30ml olive oil
4 red snapper fillets

FOR THE REFRIED BEANS:
600g black beans, soaked overnight and drained
2 onions, 1 quartered, 1 finely chopped
pinch fennel seeds
1 small bunch parsley
1 whole head garlic, halved horizontally
1 tbsp Maldon salt
50g butter
sea salt and freshly ground black pepper

TO SERVE:
fresh tomato salsa (see p. 171)
a few sprigs of coriander

1 Put the drained beans into a large saucepan with the quartered onion, fennel seeds, parsley and garlic. Cover with at least 8cm of water and simmer for 1 hour.

2 Add the salt and continue to simmer for a further 1 hour. Remove from the heat when the beans are soft and tender. Drain the beans and reserve the bean liquor.

3 Put the butter into a heavy-based pan and heat until it starts to foam.

4 Add the chopped onion and cook until it starts turning golden. Add the drained beans along with some of the bean liquor. Season with salt and pepper and simmer over a medium heat for 15 minutes.

5 Heat the olive oil in a heavy-based frying pan and fry the fish fillets until cooked.

6 Serve the fish on small mounds of the refried beans, spoon over the fresh tomato salsa and garnish with a sprig of coriander.

TIP FOR A TIPPLE
Blanche Belgian beer.

Nicky's Plaice

Howth is one of Ireland's main fishing ports. Once a fishing village in its own right, it has gradually been absorbed into Dublin but still has that small port, independent feel about it. Nine miles north-east of Dublin City, situated on the Howth peninsula, it looks out over the Irish Sea and is home to a substantial fleet of trawlers as well as some excellent fish shops and restaurants.

I was in Howth to visit Nicky McLoughlin of Nicky's Plaice, for my money one of the best fishmongers in Ireland. Surprisingly for a city the size of Dublin, it isn't easy to get good, fresh fish on a daily basis. Anyone in the know will direct you to Nicky's Plaice, at the end of West Pier in Howth. You can't miss it, as there's a large blue sign in the shape of a plaice swinging above the door. There is a strip of shops and fish restaurants along one side of West Pier, with the trawlers moored directly opposite. This is fish as fresh and local as you can get it – literally unloaded from the boats and carted right into the shop. I arrived on a Sunday, hoping to get a feel of the town when it was less busy, but the pier was heaving. It reminded me that we are an island and that fishing is our heritage – we know how to catch fish, the people here are experts in cleaning and selling it and customers will come from miles around to eat it.

Nicky McLoughlin, now in his seventies, has all the brio, humour and optimism of a true Dubliner and the energy of a man half his age. He started out as a fisherman, but when the industry was suffering he decided to hang up his nets and try his hand at fish retailing and processing. When he started in 1959, the shop was little more than a lean-to on the pier, but people were prepared to travel to get his fish because of the quality, the fair price and the guaranteed freshness.

Today, Nicky's Plaice is the oldest shop on the pier, and while the premises have changed somewhat, the quality, freshness and fair prices are the same. And the people keep coming too. I got there early on Monday morning hoping to hit a quiet time so I could talk with Nicky and his son Martin, who now runs the shop, but by 11:00 a.m. the shop was packed.

The shop is open plan. The counters are up front with the fish laid out on smashed ice. Behind the counters you can see the men in their blue shirts, white aprons and hats filleting the fish, and beyond that you look out a large window to the sea. There is a positive, buzzy vibe in the shop with plenty of banter between the men who work there and the customers. The only woman working in the shop is Jo O'Brien, who works on the till and knows everyone's name! I suspect many of the customers come in for a chat and to catch up with Jo as well as for their fish.

The shop has a reputation for passing on great recipes and always has one for the catch of the day. Behind the fish counter is a blackboard advertising the next fish cookery class, which are taught by Dario and Tom, who work in the shop. Martin was aware that there was a generation gap in cooking skills and that while many young people might like fish, they didn't know how to cook it. The cookery classes were a way to reconnect people with cooking fish while creating a new customer base at the same time.

The shop also supplies wholesale to local restaurants and shops and sells a range of delicious oak-smoked salmon and cod. One of the things I particularly like about Nicky's is that they will give you the fish heads and tails for stock and stew. Any scraps they don't get rid of they throw to the waiting seals bobbing up and down in the harbour. It's a great treat for customers' kids to be given a bucket of scraps to throw in.

I have great admiration for the McLoughlins. Their personalities and attitude make it easy to think it's all been a breeze, but it takes a great deal of work to build up a business like theirs and to stay so consistently at the top of the game. When I asked Nicky what his ethos was, he didn't hesitate to answer – he wants everyone who works for him to be happy. He believes in positive energy and combines old traditions and values with the new generation's ideas and innovations. And this is a man in his seventies. Must be all that fish!

Nicky's Plaice
West Pier, Howth, Co. Dublin
Tel: +353 (0)1 832 3557
E-mail: nickysplaice@eircom.net?
www.nickysplaice.ie

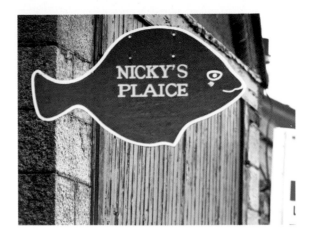

Round Fish

Round white fish such as haddock, hake, ling, huss, whiting and monkfish are firm fleshed, and as such are fantastic for taking good hearty sauces and hold their shape well in pies, fish cakes, croquettes, curries and stews.

At one point we have all either eaten or made a fish pie or cake, but fish stews aren't eaten much in Ireland, as they are in France, Spain or Italy. I want to change that, as they are so easy to make! The three key things about fish stew are the base, the stock or liquid you use and timing. Fish stew is basically a soup base to which you add the fish. To make the base, simply fry off some onions and garlic, add your herbs or spices and a little alcohol (wine, Pernod or Noilly Prat). If you're making a Mediterranean tomato-based stew, add the tomatoes now. Let the base reduce and thicken, then add your fish stock. If you're using potatoes, add them now and simmer until they're tender, then add your fish – first the firm fish, then the prawns, clams, squid, mussels, etc. Cut your fish into chunks so that they cook at the same time – the firmer the fish, the smaller the chunks. Fish stew is wonderfully adaptable. With just a few tweaks to the ingredients, you can go from a filling family meal to a sophisticated dinner party dish. For a hearty dish, try Mediterranean fish stew with potatoes, tomatoes, big chunks of white fish and shellfish. I love spicy fish stews, like the North African tagines. Just add harissa to the base and coriander and mint before you serve.

How to Fillet Round Fish

1 Lay the fish on a board with the back away from you and the head pointing to the left.
2 Lift the gill fin and cut at an angle behind the fin to the top of the head.
3 Hold the fish firmly against the board. Insert the knife at the head end and keeping the knife almost flat, cut along the top of the back of the fish to the tail.
4 About halfway down the fish, near the end of the belly cavity, push the knife blade through and over the backbone. Cut towards the tail, keeping the knife as flat to the bone as possible. Lift this part of the fillet up and, using long, sweeping strokes and keeping the knife blade almost flat, cut the top half of the fillet free from the rib cage.
5 Turn the fish over, with the head now pointing to the right. Insert the knife at the tail end and make a long cut along the top back of the fish towards the head.
6 Lift the gill fin and make an angled cut around the head.
7 Repeat the process as before, finishing by cutting the fillet free from the rib cage.

Fish Cakes with Autumn Salsa

SERVES 4

> **400g hake**
> **1 bay leaf**
> **400g mashed potato**
> **250ml olive oil, for frying**
> **1 red pepper, deseeded and finely chopped**
> **2 scallions, finely chopped**
> **juice of $^1/_2$ lemon**
> **sea salt and freshly ground black pepper**
> **1 egg yolk**
> **flour, for coating**

1 Poach the fish by placing it in a saucepan with the bay leaf, covering with water and simmering for about 10 minutes. Drain, place the hake in a large bowl with the mashed potato and mix well.

2 Place a frying pan over a medium heat and pour in a drop of olive oil. Add the red pepper and scallions and cook until soft. Stir the cooked pepper and scallions into the fish and potato mixture, then add the lemon juice and season well with salt and pepper. Bind together with the egg yolk, then divide the mixture into 4 large balls.

3 Flatten them out with your hands into circular shapes. Dip the fish cakes into a bowl of seasoned flour and flip them back and forth in your hands to shake off any excess flour.

4 Put the frying pan back on the heat, add a generous splash of olive oil and fry the fish cakes, turning when they are golden brown beneath. This should take about 3 minutes per side. Serve with the delicious autumn salsa (see overleaf).

FOR THE SPICY AUTUMN SALSA:
olive oil
4 ripe plum tomatoes
1 red chilli, seeds removed
1 red pepper, quartered and seeds removed
1 garlic clove, crushed
50g toasted almonds
sea salt and freshly ground black pepper

1   Place a small saucepan over a medium heat and add a dollop of olive oil.
2   Dice the tomatoes, chilli and red pepper. Add the chilli, red pepper and crushed garlic to the pan and leave to simmer for 2 minutes. Add the chopped tomatoes and toasted almonds and season with salt and pepper. Lower the heat and allow to simmer for 10 minutes.
3   You can add fresh basil or coriander at the end if you wish.

VARIATIONS

Spicy Fish Cakes
• Replace the red pepper with 2 more red chillies, deseeded and finely chopped.
• Replace the almonds with 1 tsp ground cumin.
• Fold in 1 tbsp finely chopped fresh coriander.

TIP FOR A TIPPLE
Fish pie and fish cakes are perfect with an Albariño from northern Spain.

Perfect Family Fish Pie

SERVES 4

I hope you will use this recipe a lot, as it doesn't need many ingredients, is simple and fast to make and all the family will love it.

butter
600g haddock, hake, whiting or ling
sea salt and freshly ground black pepper
1 tbsp Dijon mustard
150ml cream
450g mashed potato

1   Preheat the oven to 180°C.
2   Grease a roasting dish with butter.
3   Cut the fish up into small pieces and place in the bottom of the roasting dish. Season well with salt and pepper.
4   Smear the fish with the Dijon mustard and pour over the cream.
5   Spread the mashed potato on top and dot over small cubes of butter.
6   Bake in the preheated oven for 30–40 minutes, until golden brown and piping hot.

VARIATIONS

Prawn and Pea Fish Pie
• Add 10 cooked prawns over the fish.
• Fold 100g of defrosted peas into the mashed potatoes.

Hake Seared in a Sun-dried Tomato Tapenade

SERVES 2

I use hake for this recipe, but you can use any firm white round fish fillet.

**2 hake fillets
sea salt and freshly ground black pepper
olive oil**

**FOR THE SUN-DRIED TOMATO TAPENADE:
200g semi sun-dried tomatoes
80g freshly grated Parmesan
150ml olive oil
1 garlic clove
70g pine nuts**

1 Preheat the oven to 190°C.
2 Make the sun-dried tomato pesto by placing all the ingredients in a blender and whizzing for 3 minutes.
3 Season the hake fillets with salt and pepper. Smear the skin side with the pesto.
4 Put a frying pan over a high heat and add a dollop of olive oil. After 1 minute, place the hake fillets in the pan, skin side up, and leave to cook for 2 minutes. Then place the pan in the preheated oven for 10 minutes. Serve straight away.

TIP FOR A TIPPLE
This dish is delicious with a glass of Traminer from Germany.

Kedgeree

SERVES 4

This is a traditional British dish that is served for brunch. I love it because it's delicious, hearty, healthy and you can make it in large quantities if you have lots of guests.

200g rice
300g white fish (haddock, hake, ling)
milk
100g butter
1 onion, diced
2 tsp curry powder
sea salt and freshly ground black pepper
2 eggs, hardboiled and sliced
2 tbsp chopped fresh flat leaf parsley

1   Cook the rice in a saucepan of hot water for 15 minutes, or until cooked.

2   While the rice is cooking, place the fish in a saucepan, cover with milk and simmer for 10 minutes. Remove and drain.

3   Place the saucepan back over a low heat and drop in the butter. Once melted, stir in the onion, cover and allow to sweat for 5 minutes. Remove the lid and stir in the curry powder.

4   Flake the fish and stir into the onions, followed by the cooked rice. Season with salt and pepper.

5   Tip the rice and fish mixture into a warm serving dish and scatter the sliced hardboiled eggs and parsley on top.

TIP FOR A TIPPLE
Fumé Blanc from northern Lyon is great with kedgeree.

Poached Monkfish with Basil Hollandaise Sauce

SERVES 4

I learned this dish when I was a chef at Ballymaloe House. Rory O'Connell was the head chef while I was there and his patience, knowledge, style and passion inspired me so much. This recipe is a classic French way of cooking monkfish.

4 monkfish fillets (weighing approx. 200g each)

FOR THE BASIL HOLLANDAISE:
3 egg yolks
1 ice cube
180g butter, cubed
juice of ¹/₂ lemon
2 tbsp shredded fresh basil

1   Cut the monkfish fillets into 3cm pieces. Place in a saucepan of boiling salted water and simmer for 5 minutes.

2   While the monkfish is cooking, make the hollandaise sauce. Place a glass or Pyrex bowl over a saucepan of simmering water. Place the egg yolks and 1 ice cube in the bowl and whisk gently. Add the butter one cube at a time, whisking constantly and adding another cube when the previous one has melted. Once all the butter has melted, remove the bowl from the saucepan and whisk in the lemon juice and fresh basil. Season with salt and pepper.

3   Drain the monkfish from the water and arrange on serving plates. Cover with the basil hollandaise and serve immediately.

TIP FOR A TIPPLE
Try a Pouilly-Fumé from southern Burgundy for this classic monkfish and hollandaise.

Moroccan Monkfish Tagine

SERVES 6

I love Moroccan food, and in 2007 I took my first trip to Marrakesh in Morocco. As I walked through the markets, I could smell delicious spicy flavours lingering in the air, leading me to a tiny canteen-like café that had one dish on the menu – fish tagine. It was everything I had dreamed of, and as I ate I scribbled the ingredients on a piece of paper so that every time I want a taste of Marrakesh I dust off my tagine and spice up my fish.

olive oil
100g flour, seasoned with salt and pepper
1kg monkfish, skinned and sliced into 3cm pieces
2 onions, diced
3 garlic cloves, crushed
1 large red chilli, deseeded and finely diced
1 tsp ground cumin
1 tsp paprika
1 tsp ground fennel seeds
5 plum tomatoes (if fresh, skinned)
5cm fresh ginger, peeled and grated
1 litre fish stock
4 preserved lemons (optional), sliced
1 tbsp tomato purée
bunch of fresh coriander, chopped
sea salt and freshly ground black pepper

1 Preheat the oven to 170°C.

2 Place a frying pan over a low heat and add a dollop of olive oil.

3 While the oil is warming, tip the flour into a bowl and lightly dust the pieces of monkfish in the flour.

4 Drop the flour-dusted monkfish into the pan. Sauté on each side for just 1 minute and transfer to a dish.

5 Once all the fish has been sautéed, add the onions, garlic, chilli, spices and ginger to the pan. Cover and leave to sweat for 5 minutes.

6 Stir in the tomatoes, fish stock, sliced preserved lemons (optional) and tomato purée with the onions and spices and leave to cook for 10 minutes.

7 Pour the spicy tomato liquid into a casserole, stir in the fish and season with salt and pepper.

8 Cook in the preheated oven for 15 minutes.

9 Just before serving, stir in the fresh coriander. Serve with couscous (see p. 183).

TIP FOR A TIPPLE
Gewürztraminer from the Rhine region is delicious with this spicy tagine.

Overlooking Clonakilty Bay in the lovely fishing village of Ring, you'll find **Deasy's Pub and Restaurant.** *Chef Kaitlin Ruth is a chef I have followed and loved for years. In my opinion, she is one of the most underrated chefs in Ireland. Her cooking is magical and her passion for food is contagious. She orders her fish directly from the local fishermen, so the menu changes every day, but what a menu she creates! Her chowder was perfected after a three-month stint in New England to find the perfect recipe. Anything she creates has a story behind it, whether it be simply seared scallops wrapped in prosciutto or a Moroccan fish tagine. The menu may change, but one thing that stays the same is her fabulous cooking. Deasy's Harbour Bar and Seafood Restaurant, Ring Village, Clonakilty, Co Cork. Tel: +353 (0)23 35741.*

Baked Red Mullet with Lemon and Dill

SERVES 2

3 red mullet
2 lemons, sliced into half-moon shapes
3 sprigs fresh dill
sea salt and freshly ground black pepper
olive oil

1 Preheat the oven to 220°C.

2 Clean and gut the red mullet and pat them dry.

3 Make 3 light slits on one side of the fish. This allows the flavours to get into the fish.

4 Lay half the lemon slices in a roasting dish and place the red mullet on top. Place another slice of lemon on each mullet and lay a sprig of dill on each.

5 Season with salt and pepper and a good drizzle of olive oil. Pop in the preheated oven for 15 minutes.

6 When cooked, pour all the remaining juices from the pan over the fish before you serve.

TIP FOR A TIPPLE
Catarratto from Sicily is a classic match for the mullet.

Indian Spiced Ling

SERVES 4

This recipe is also great using monkfish, hake, haddock or whiting and is delicious served with a raita.

1 tsp ground cumin
1 tsp ground coriander
$^1/_2$ tsp ground turmeric
$^1/_2$ tsp curry powder
150g tomato passata
200ml water

olive oil
10 curry leaves
1 red chilli, left whole
500g ling fillets, cut into 5cm pieces
lime wedges, to serve
basmati rice, to serve

1 Place all the spices in a bowl and mix together with the passata and water.
2 Place a large frying pan or casserole dish over a medium heat and pour in a good dollop of olive oil.
3 Add the curry leaves, whole chilli and tomato mixture and leave to cook for 10 minutes.
4 Stir the fish into the pan and leave to cook for 5–8 minutes. Serve with lime wedges and basmati rice.

Raita

SERVES 4

$^1/_2$ medium cucumber
150ml natural yoghurt
$^1/_2$ tsp cumin seeds
2 tbsp fresh mint, chopped

1 Chop the cucumber into small dice (about 0.5cm).
2 Mix together the cucumber, yoghurt, cumin and fresh mint in a bowl.

TIP FOR A TIPPLE
Fumé Blanc from northern Lyon is great with the Indian spices.

Fish Stew with Almonds and Saffron

SERVES 4–6, DEPENDING ON HOW HUNGRY YOUR GUESTS ARE!

olive oil
800g white fish (ling, haddock, hake or whiting), cut into small pieces
sea salt and freshly ground black pepper
1 onion, finely chopped
3 large tomatoes, diced (or 3 large tinned plum tomatoes)
2 tbsp finely chopped almonds
3 garlic cloves
a few threads of saffron
500ml white wine
2 tbsp finely chopped fresh parsley

1 Preheat the oven to 175°C.
2 Place a frying pan over a medium heat and add a dollop of olive oil. Add the pieces of fish, season with salt and pepper and cook for just 30 seconds on each side. Transfer to a casserole dish.
3 Sweat the onions in the pan for 5 minutes, then add the tomatoes. Cook for a further 5 minutes and transfer to the casserole dish.
4 Grind the almonds, garlic and saffron threads together in a pestle and mortar and stir into the casserole, followed by the wine, finely chopped parsley and 1 glass of water.
5 Cook in the preheated oven for 20 minutes. Serve with rice.

TIP FOR A TIPPLE
A Pinot Noir from Burgundy is beautiful with the almonds and saffron.

Cacciucco Soup from Livorno

SERVES 4

This soup is famous in the Tuscany region, in particular the town of Livorno. I live about three hours from there, and every now and again I get a serious craving, and myself and a few food-loving friends will jump on a train to Livorno in search of the cacciucco soup! But now I finally have the recipe so these cravings are met a little easier!

500g white fish fillets (ling, haddock, whiting, hake, pollock), but hold on to the bones
250g prawns or shrimp (de-shelled, but hold on to the shells)
1 carrot, peeled and sliced
1 onion, peeled and sliced
$^1/_2$ stalk of celery, sliced
olive oil
2 garlic cloves, crushed
1 red chilli, deseeded and diced
3 sage leaves
1 glass white wine
1 tbsp tomato purée
250g squid, cleaned and sliced
250g mixed mussels and clams
6 slices of sourdough bread
100ml extra virgin olive oil
sea salt and freshly ground black pepper

1 Preheat the oven to 180°C.
2 First make the fish broth/stock by placing the fish bones, prawn and shrimp shells, carrot, onion and celery in a large saucepan and covering with cold water. Bring to the boil and simmer for 20 minutes, then strain through a sieve.
3 While the stock is simmering, place a large pan over a low heat and drizzle in a dollop of olive oil followed by the garlic, diced chilli and the sage. Leave to cook for 1 minute.
4 Add the white wine and tomato purée to the pan, followed by the squid. Stir and leave to simmer for 15 minutes.
5 Add the white fish and enough fish broth to completely cover plus a bit more. Continue to cook for 5 minutes, or until the squid is tender.
6 Tip in the shellfish, cover and cook for 5 minutes, or until all the shells have opened.

7   At this point, place the sliced sourdough bread on a baking tray, season with salt and pepper and rub with extra virgin olive oil. Place in the preheated oven for 5 minutes.

8   Arrange 6 soup bowls and place 1 slice of the toasted bread at the bottom of each bowl. Pour the soup on top of the bread and serve.

TIP FOR A TIPPLE

I order Chianti from Tuscany or Vermentino from Sardinia with this soup.

Decadent Fish Croquettes

SERVES 4

These are fabulous party food. They are quite 1980s in food culture terms, but I love them anyway!

400g white fish, cooked and flaked
1 tsp finely chopped parsley
1 tsp cayenne pepper
sea salt and freshly ground black pepper
100ml Mornay sauce (see p. 169)
1 egg, beaten
200g fine breadcrumbs
olive oil

1 Place the fish, parsley, cayenne, salt and pepper in a bowl. Pour over the Mornay sauce while it's still warm and mix well. Set aside and allow to cool.

2 Scoop up the mixture using a tablespoon and form it into cork-like shapes. Lay the croquettes on a tray.

3 Using a pastry brush, gloss the croquettes with the beaten egg.

4 Scatter the fine breadcrumbs on a large plate and, one by one, gently roll the croquettes in the crumbs.

5 Fry the croquettes in a deep frying pan with hot oil for about 10 minutes, turning them over after about 5 minutes. Alternatively, bake in a preheated oven at 200°C for 15 minutes.

TIP FOR A TIPPLE
Serve an Albariño from northern Spain with these decadent croquettes.

Karen's Cullen Skink

SERVES 4

Every time I'm in London, I stay with one of my best friends, Karen McLaughlin. She is a fabulously talented scriptwriter and also a great cook. She lives right next door to the Borough Market, so we always wander down to pick up delicious ingredients, then open a bottle of wine, cook and catch up. This is the last recipe that she cooked for me, a great traditional Scottish soup that she used to eat growing up in Scotland.

> 1 large piece of smoked haddock
> 1 onion, finely chopped
> 1 bay leaf
> sea salt and freshly ground black pepper
> 900ml milk
> 200g mashed potato
> 50g butter
> chopped parsley

1 Cover the smoked haddock with water in a shallow pan, skin side down. Bring to the boil and simmer for 4–5 minutes, turning once.

2 Take the haddock from the pan and remove the skin and bones. Break up the fish into flakes, return to the cooking water and add the chopped onion, bay leaf, salt and pepper. Simmer for another 15 minutes, then strain. Discard the bay leaf but retain the stock and fish.

3 Add the milk to the fish stock and bring it back to the boil.

4 Add enough mashed potato to create the consistency you prefer (don't be afraid to make it rich and thick). Add the fish and reheat. Check for seasoning.

5 Just before serving, add the butter in small pieces so that it runs through the soup. Serve with chopped parsley on top, accompanied by triangles of toast.

Chinese Delicate Fish Rolls

SERVES 2

> 1 egg yolk
> sea salt and freshly ground black pepper
> 50g rice flour
> 50ml water
> 8 rounds of rice paper
> 200g white fish, skinless, cut into 5cm strips
> vegetable oil, for frying

> **FOR DIPPING SAUCE:**
> 50ml rice vinegar (not seasoned)
> 50ml Thai fish sauce (nam pla)
> 40g sugar
> 50ml water

1 Put the egg yolk in a bowl, season with salt and pepper and whisk.

2 In another bowl, whisk together the rice flour and water. Dip the rice paper into the bowl of the rice flour mixture, then place on a sheet of greaseproof paper.

3 Dip a piece of fish in the egg yolk and place on the edge of the rice paper. Roll the fish up in the rice paper and fold in the sides. Repeat with the remaining fish pieces.

4 Place a deep frying pan over a medium heat and fill halfway with oil.

5 Once the oil is hot, add the fish rolls with a spoon. Turn once, until light golden, and remove from the pan once the rolls are golden all over.

6 Make the dipping sauce by simply mixing all the ingredients together.

7 Serve the fish rolls warm with a bowl of the dipping sauce.

TIP FOR A TIPPLE
Serve a delicate Viognier with the fish rolls.

Thai Fish Curry

SERVES 4

    6 hot green chillies, deseeded and sliced
    2 $^1/_2$cm piece of fresh ginger, peeled and grated
    3 garlic cloves, crushed
    1 tsp ground cumin
    1 tsp ground coriander
    1 tsp ground turmeric
    1 tbsp peanut oil
    1 onion, sliced
    500ml coconut milk
    1 tbsp Thai fish sauce (nam pla)
    1 stalk of lemon grass, peeled and thinly sliced
    4 kaffir lime leaves
    800g white fish (haddock, hake or other firm fish)
    2 tbsp chopped fresh coriander
    limes wedges, to serve
    jasmine rice, to serve

1. Place the chillies, fresh ginger, garlic, cumin, ground coriander and turmeric and a drop of water in a food processor and blend.
2. Put a casserole dish, wok or a saucepan over a medium heat and pour in the peanut oil, followed by the sliced onion. Leave to cook for 1 minute, then stir in the spice blend and leave to cook for 2 more minutes.
3. Pour in the coconut milk, fish sauce, lemon grass and kaffir lime leaves and simmer for 10 minutes.
4. Stir in the pieces of fish, making sure they are well coated in the curry.
5. Leave to simmer for approximately 15 minutes, or until the fish is cooked.
6. Stir in the fresh coriander just before serving.
7. Serve with a bowl of jasmine rice and lime wedges.

TIP FOR A TIPPLE
A pale ale or a light blonde beer is delicious with a Thai fish curry.

Smoked Haddock Chowder

SERVES 4

When it's a cold, rainy day I love nothing more than to cook a warming fish chowder. You can add lardons of bacon if you wish.

15g butter
1 onion, diced
1 leek, finely sliced
1 garlic clove, crushed
splash of white wine
300ml fish stock (see p. 53)
200ml milk
200g potatoes, peeled and diced
500g smoked haddock, skin removed and cut into small chunks
150ml double cream
bunch of fresh chives, chopped
sea salt and freshly ground black pepper
crusty bread, to serve

1 Place a saucepan over a low heat and add the butter. Once the butter has melted, stir in the onion, leeks and garlic. Cover and leave to sweat for 3 minutes.

2 Remove the lid, pour in the white wine and cook for a further 3 minutes.

3 Pour in the stock, turn up the heat and bring to the boil.

4 Reduce the heat to a simmer and add in the potatoes. Leave to cook for 10 minutes.

5 Using a large spoon, add in the pieces of smoked fish and leave for 5 minutes.

6 Stir in the cream and chopped chives and season with salt and pepper. Leave to cook for a further 1 minute. Serve with warmed crusty bread.

TIP FOR A TIPPLE

For a smoky chowder, try a Chardonnay from California.

Spiced Swordfish Steaks

SERVES 2

2 tsp ground coriander
2 tsp cayenne
$^1/_2$ tsp turmeric
1 tsp ground cumin
juice and zest of 1 lime
2 swordfish steaks
sea salt and freshly ground black pepper
olive oil
lime wedges, to serve
couscous salad, to serve (see p. 183)

1 Mix the spices, lime juice and zest with 1 tbsp water.

2 Place the swordfish steaks in a dish and coat them with the spice mixture. Season with salt and pepper and place in a fridge to marinate for 30 minutes.

3 Place a griddle or frying pan over a medium heat and, once hot, add a dollop of olive oil.

4 Place the swordfish steaks in the pan, reduce the heat to medium and cook for 6 minutes. Turn the fish over and cook for a further 6 minutes.

5 Serve with lime wedges and a couscous salad (see p. 183).

TIP FOR A TIPPLE
Grenache holds its own with the spicy swordfish steak.

Bouillabaisse

SERVES 8

Just a couple of months ago, I took the train from Turin (where I live in northern Italy) to Paris. It was a nine-hour train ride and I arrived at 7:00 p.m., tired and hungry but equally excited to be in this wonderful city. Before I checked into my hotel, I popped into a bistro and was given this delicious French classic fish stew. It's creamy, intense, hearty and so, so delicious.

olive oil
2 onions, peeled and sliced
2 garlic cloves, crushed
1 fennel bulb, sliced
2 sprigs fresh thyme
1 bay leaf
800g potatoes, peeled and
  sliced
sea salt and freshly ground
  black pepper
500g tomatoes, peeled and
  sliced
2kg mixed fish such as haddock, monkfish, sea bass, red

snapper, halibut, squid, etc.
2 litres fish stock
100ml Pernod
pinch of saffron threads
1 baguette

FOR THE ROUILLE:
3 tbsp fish stock
pinch of saffron threads
2 garlic cloves
200ml mayonnaise
pinch of saffron and cayenne
  pepper

1 Preheat the oven to 180°C.
2 Place a large pot over a medium heat and add in a good dollop of olive oil.
3 Tip the onions, garlic, fennel, thyme, bay leaf and potatoes into the pot and season with salt and pepper. After a couple of minutes, stir in the tomatoes and leave to cook for another 2 minutes.
4 Add in the fish pieces, followed by the fish stock, Pernod and saffron. Season with salt and pepper and simmer for 10 minutes, or until the fish is cooked.
5 While the fish is cooking, slice the baguette, brush with olive oil and place in the preheated oven for 10 minutes.
6 Make the rouille by simply placing all the ingredients in a food processor and blending.
7 To serve, ladle the soup into warm bowls and place a slice of toasted baguette on top with a dollop of rouille.

TIP FOR A TIPPLE
Rosé from Provence is wonderful with bouillabaisse.

Spicy Autumn Fish Stew

SERVES 4

olive oil
1 onion, diced
2 celery stalks, thinly sliced
3 garlic cloves, crushed
1 tbsp coriander seeds, roughly crushed
1 tsp ground cumin
1 bay leaf
sprig fresh thyme
2 x 400g tins tinned chopped tomatoes
125ml red wine
300ml fish stock
sea salt and freshly ground black pepper
1kg mixed fish fillets, cut into small pieces
mashed potato, polenta or rice, to serve

1 Place a casserole dish over a medium heat and pour in a dollop of olive oil, followed by the onion and celery. Leave to cook for 5 minutes.

2 Add the garlic, coriander, cumin, bay leaf and thyme. Cook for a further 2 minutes.

3 Stir in the tomatoes and leave to reduce and thicken for about 10 minutes.

4 Pour in the wine, bring back to the boil and cook for 1 minute. Then add the stock, season with salt and pepper and leave to simmer for 15–20 minutes.

5 Add all the fish to the stew and stir well. Simmer gently for about 5 minutes. Serve with creamy mashed potatoes, polenta or rice.

TIP FOR A TIPPLE
Try a Russane with the autumn fish stew.

SALLY BARNES

I am often impressed by a certain producer or astounded by a particular product, but it isn't often that you meet a producer as wild and wonderful as the food they produce. Not so Sally Barnes of the Woodcock Smokery near Castletownsend in West Cork. The first thing she would tell you about her smoked fish is that it is wild, caught locally by fishermen who adhere to sustainable fishing practices. I heard her talk at the Taste of Cork festival and she attributed the success of her award-winning salmon, which has been acclaimed worldwide, to two things: the quality of the fish and the fact that every stage of the process, from filleting to slicing, is done by hand. She remembers that the first time she ever filleted a fish it took her 40 minutes, she was so afraid of damaging it. Today she can fillet a fish in minutes, but the care and respect for the fish and her craft remain, which is what sets her product apart. She told me that she thinks of every fish she receives as an individual, and now that it's dead it's her job to give it the best possible send-off.

Even the wood chips she uses to smoke the fish are sourced locally and she only uses wood from indigenous trees. Much of her wood is bartered from local furniture makers for a side of salmon. She ensures she gets good wood by telling each one that the fish they get will be smoked over the wood they supply. That way, she can be sure there will be no glue or nails in it, as 'people take care of their tummies'.

When I went to meet Sally, a journalist from *Rolling Stone* magazine had just arrived, and an Italian who had come for a month but stayed for three ('he brought a crate of very good wine') had just left. There is a constant flow of people through the old stone farmhouse. Sally is always interested in people and they are attracted by her charisma. But it's the sea that is her enduring love and that she has dedicated her life to.

Originally from Ayrshire, she came to West Cork in 1975 when she married an Irish fisherman. In those days, she went out on the boats, the only woman in Cork doing so at the time, to my knowledge, in an open 50-foot boat with an outboard motor going eight or nine miles out to sea. She also made the tangle nets that they caught the turbot, monkfish and crayfish with. It was a hard life. There was enormous pressure to sell the fish the day you caught it because the price fell steeply the day after. Her change of career happened by accident rather than design. A client who owed them £1,500 was ordered by the court to pay the money back at £5 a week. The client gave them a tenth of the money up front and a kiln.

At first Sally just smoked trout for her family to eat, but when she became pregnant with her daughter, Joleine (who now works full time alongside her mum at the smokery) and couldn't go out on the boat, she started taking the fish smoking seriously. When we visited to take photos for the book I was surprised by how small the smokery is. While Alberto took the photos, I sat in the kitchen with Sally, tasting and talking about fish. The salmon was velvety and melt-in-your-mouth smooth, while the texture is slightly drier than farmed salmon because there is less fat. The taste was intense and completely delicious. While we were chatting, Alan Murray, a fellow Scot who works in the smokery with Sally, brought in some freshly smoked kipper. It was so smooth that I honestly thought he had added cream, but it was simply the natural juices of the fish. Gorgeous.

Sally invited Alberto and me to see the band Dogtail Soup at Skibbereen Community Hall. At the end of the gig, Sally pulled out a side of salmon that the lead singer had ordered online while touring in France. It struck me that I had never seen Sally without her fish – it is so much a part of her.

Sally first trained to be a teacher, and that ethos is still with her. She sees her future as educating people about the sea and fish. At the moment, she is converting the farmhouse so that people can come and stay for a week or two to learn about fish and smoking fish. She also wants to travel and lecture – whatever it takes to make people more aware.

Although it's the salmon that has given Sally worldwide acclaim, she also smokes other fish, including mackerel, herring, tuna, haddock and pollock using both hot and cold smoking techniques. I was blown away by her hot smoked tuna, which she uses to make a mean carbonara, replacing the pancetta with tuna.

I have included the tuna carbonara recipe in this book (see p. 141) as a tribute to a wild woman who makes the best wild smoked salmon in the world.

Woodcock Smokery
Gortbrack, Castletownsend, Skibbereen, Co. Cork
Tel: (+353) 028 36232
E-mail: sally@woodcocksmokery.com
www.woodcocksmokery.com

Oily Fish

Oily fish are the ones we are always encouraged to eat because of their high omega 3 content. Omega 3 essential fatty acids are associated with preventing or reducing the effects of a wide range of illnesses and diseases, including heart disease, strokes, cancer, lupus, arthritis and many more. A lot of research is also being done into the positive effects of omega 3 oils on depression.

Oily fish includes salmon, mackerel, herring, trout, tuna, anchovies and sardines. These fish work really well with sharp citrusy flavours that cut their oiliness and richness. Salmon and sardines both work well on the barbecue and make a healthy alternative to burgers and sausages. The robust oily fish also hold their shape well when cooked. Because of their strong taste, they can cope with strong spicy flavours like chilli, horseradish and olives. Remember mackerel pâté? A little butter, horseradish, sour cream, a blender and away you go – it couldn't be easier or more delicious. I love herring dipped in egg, rolled in oats and fried in butter – the crispy coat and light texture of the fish combined with the rich taste are an absolute winner. Try salmon, trout and sardines on the barbecue; they are wonderful with a crisp, fresh salad and a glass of chilled wine.

Smoked Salmon Mousse

SERVES 4 AS A STARTER

I first fell in love with smoked salmon mousse when I had a stall at the Midleton farmers' market next to Frank Hederman of Belvelly Smokehouse. I love Frank's smoked fish, and his smoked salmon mousse is to live and die for. There would be queues every Saturday morning at his stall and the first thing to go would be the mousse. He used to kindly let me clean the bowl with a piece of Arbutus sourdough bread and it was the highlight of my week. Here is the closest I can come to his mousse.

> **250g smoked salmon**
> **100g cream cheese**
> **50g crème fraîche**
> **juice of 1 lemon**
> **sea salt and freshly ground black pepper, to taste**
> **Irish soda bread, to serve**

1 Place all the ingredients in a food processor and whizz until the mixture reaches a smooth consistency. Serve with toasted Irish soda bread.

VARIATIONS

Smoked Salmon and Caper Mousse

• Add 1 tsp drained and rinsed capers before you blend.

Mackerel and Lemon Mousse

• Replace the smoked salmon with smoked mackerel.

Marinated Salmon in Mint and Lemon

SERVES 2

> **2 x 200g salmon fillets, skinned and pin-boned**
> **juice of 1 lemon**
> **2 sprigs mint, roughly chopped**
> **sea salt and freshly ground black pepper**
> **1 tbsp olive oil**
> **cucumber and dill pickle, to serve (see p. 136)**
> **creamy lemon potato salad, to serve (see p. 182)**

1 Place the salmon fillets in a bowl, pour over the lemon juice and chopped mint and season with salt and pepper. Mix well, cover and place in a fridge for 1–3 hours.

2 Place your griddle pan (or frying pan or barbecue) over a medium heat and add the olive oil. When the oil is hot, remove the salmon from the fridge and place it straight on the griddle. Cook for 3 minutes on each side.

3 Serve the marinated salmon with a cucumber and dill pickle (see p. 136) and a creamy lemon potato salad (see p. 183).

Grilled Salmon with a Lime, Yoghurt and Honey Sauce

SERVES 4

When wild salmon is in season, there's no other fish that can compare to its incredible flavour. When it's not in season, I suggest you use trout for this recipe. The lime, yoghurt and honey sauce also goes very well with grilled tuna. Perfect for cooking at the beach or on a barbecue.

4 salmon fillets
sea salt and freshly ground black pepper
juice of 1 lime
olive oil
boiled baby potatoes, to serve

FOR THE LIME, YOGURT AND HONEY SAUCE:
200g Greek yoghurt
juice and zest of 1 lime
1 tsp honey

1 Season the salmon with salt and pepper and pour the lime juice over all the fillets.

2 Place a griddle or frying pan over a medium heat and once warm, add a dollop of olive oil. Wait for about 30 seconds, then add the salmon fillets and cook for 4 minutes. Turn the fillets over and cook for a further 4 minutes.

3 While the salmon is cooking, make the sauce by simply mixing all the ingredients in a bowl.

4 Serve each fillet with a good dollop of the yoghurt sauce and some boiled baby potatoes.

Smoked Salmon with Gooey Poached Eggs and Creamy Crème Fraîche

SERVES 2

So delicious to eat on a lazy Sunday morning with a pot of coffee, the Sunday papers and good company.

4 organic or free-range eggs
100ml crème fraîche
4 sprigs chives, finely chopped
100g wild smoked salmon, thinly sliced
sea salt and freshly ground black pepper
toasted brioche, to serve

1 Place a saucepan of salted water on to boil.

2 When the water has come to the boil, stir the water with a spoon. While the water is still swirling, break in your eggs as close to the water as possible (the swirling water and breaking the eggs close to the water both help to form the perfect poached egg).

3 Reduce the heat and allow the eggs to poach for 4 minutes. Remove with a slotted spoon and drain on a plate.

4 Wrap each egg in a slice of smoked salmon, place a dollop of crème fraîche on top and sprinkle with the finely chopped chives.

5 Season with salt and pepper and serve with toasted brioche.

TIP: You can also use scrambled eggs for this recipe instead of poached eggs. Just make sure you add a little knob of butter to the scrambled eggs before you take them off the heat.

Mackerel Baked with Rosemary and Potatoes

SERVES 2

I love this recipe – the juices and oils from the mackerel trickle down into the baby potatoes and the rosemary adds a delicate but sweet flavouring to the fish.

8 baby potatoes
2 whole fresh mackerel
1 red onion, sliced into half moons
sea salt and freshly ground black pepper
1 sprig fresh rosemary
olive oil
rocket salsa, to serve

1   Preheat the oven to 200°C.
2   Scrub the baby potatoes (but leave the skins on) and cut into slices.
3   Wash the fresh mackerel and pat dry. Open up the cavity and line with potato slices and the sliced red onion. Season with salt and pepper and lie the fresh sprig of rosemary on top. Tie together with a string of kitchen twine.
4   Put the remaining potato and red onion slices in a roasting dish and place the mackerel on top. Drizzle a good dollop of olive oil over the fish and potatoes.
5   Cook in the preheated oven for 15 minutes. Delicious served with a rocket salsa.

Rocket Salsa

SERVES 2

1 large bunch rocket, finely chopped
1 small red tiger chilli, finely chopped
2 tbsp extra virgin olive oil
juice of 1 lemon
sea salt and freshly ground black pepper

1   Place the rocket and chilli in a bowl and stir in the olive oil and lemon juice.
2   Season with salt and pepper and mix well.

Mackerel with Beetroot and Horseradish

SERVES 2

Mackerel is a powerful fish in that it can stand up to other strong ingredients. The sweetness of the beetroot and the intense, deep flavour of the horseradish coated over the crispy, oily fish is heavenly.

knob of butter
2 mackerel, filleted
sea salt and freshly ground black pepper
1 lemon, cut into wedges

FOR THE BEETROOT AND HORSERADISH:
1 beetroot, boiled and grated
5cm piece of fresh horseradish, grated, or 100ml fresh horseradish sauce
4 tbsp crème fraîche
squeeze of fresh lemon juice
lemon wedges, to serve

1 For the mackerel, heat the butter in a frying pan over a high heat and add the mackerel fillets, skin side down. Season with salt and pepper and fry for 2 minutes. Turn over and fry for a further 2 minutes.

2 For the beetroot and horseradish, simply mix together all the ingredients and season to taste.

3 Serve the mackerel with a generous dollop of the beetroot and horseradish and a wedge of lemon.

Smoked Mackerel and Horseradish Pâté

SERVES 4 AS A STARTER

I love to serve this pâté in small pots with melba toast. You can also store it in a Kilner jar to have at hand for lunch or to bring to someone's house as a gift.

400g smoked mackerel
200g crème fraîche
5cm piece of fresh horseradish
juice of 1 lemon
freshly ground black pepper

1 Crumble up the smoked mackerel and put into a food processor.
2 Add the rest of the ingredients and blend until you reach a smooth consistency. Serve with hot toast.

Chilli Fried Mackerel

SERVES 2

I got my love of mackerel from my mum, Irene. She grew up in the fishing town of Cobh, Co. Cork, where her father was a fisherman. During her summer holidays as a child, she would help her father on the boats. She has recounted many stories of being on the boat with him, but one that is imbedded in my mind is her lying back on my grandfather's boat, dreamily looking up at the clouds and her hand held tight to a string line, waiting for the tug of a mackerel. The tug would come and she would pull the fish out of the sea and hold onto it like a baby until they pulled up to the slipway at the back of their house. That night, my grandmother, Rita, would dab the mackerel in a bit of flour and fry it in butter and my mum would treasure every last bite. I add a little chilli to my fried mackerel, as I love the way the fire cuts through the oiliness of the fish.

50g butter
1 chilli, deseeded and finely chopped
1 garlic clove, crushed
4 fresh mackerel fillets
sea salt and freshly ground black pepper
juice of 1 lemon

1   Heat a frying pan and drop in the butter, chilli and garlic.
2   Once the chilli butter begins to foam, add the mackerel, skin down, for 2 minutes. Season with salt and pepper, turn the fish over, squeeze the lemon juice over the fish and cook for a further 2 minutes.
3   Remove to a plate and drizzle the chilli butter over the fillets.

Whole Poached Sea Trout

SERVES 4–6

I love having a lunch party on a Saturday afternoon in the summertime. Poached sea trout is the perfect fish to serve, along with some cucumber pickle, salads and a homemade mayonnaise.

1 x approx. 1.5kg sea trout, cleaned and de-scaled
water
sea salt
bay leaf
homemade mayonnaise, to serve (see p. 170)

1 Pour 3 litres of cold water and 3 tbsp of sea salt into a fish kettle (or a large saucepan) and bring it to the boil.

2 Gently add in the sea trout and a bay leaf, making sure that the water covers all the fish. Leave to simmer for 20 minutes. Drain off the water and allow the trout to drain free of any water.

3 Remove the skin and the fins. Serve with cucumber and dill pickle (below) and a bowl of homemade mayonnaise (p. 170).

Summer Cucumber and Dill Pickle

MAKES APPROX. 400ML

1 cucumber
1 onion, peeled
1 tbsp chopped fresh dill
80g white granulated sugar
250ml cider vinegar
1 tsp salt

1 Using a mandolin or sharp knife, thinly slice the cucumber and onion into a large bowl and mix in the fresh dill.

2 Pour the sugar, vinegar and salt over the cucumber and onion. Cover with a towel and leave for about 2 hours.

3 Give the cucumber and dill pickle a good stir and leave for another hour. Store in an airtight container or screw-top jar.

VARIATIONS

Poached Wild Salmon
- Replace the trout with wild salmon.

Chilli Cucumber Pickle
- Add 1 tsp of finely chopped red chilli to the pickle.

Cucumber and Mustard Seed Pickle
- Add 1 tsp of yellow mustard seeds to the pickle.

Mediterranean Crusted Trout

SERVES 4

This is a great recipe that can be used for many different types of fish, such as hake, haddock or salmon. I love the juicy flavours of the tomatoes and olives running through the trout. It's perfect at any time of the year for a little taste of the Mediterranean.

100g fresh breadcrumbs
55g black pitted olives, finely chopped
1 tbsp finely chopped fresh parsley
1 tbsp finely chopped fresh thyme
2 plum tomatoes, finely chopped (good tinned ones will do fine)
sea salt and freshly ground black pepper
olive oil
4 x 150g trout fillets
rice, couscous or potatoes, to serve

1 Preheat the oven to 180°C.

2 Place the breadcrumbs, olives, herbs and tomatoes in a large bowl. Season with salt and pepper and mix well.

3 Line a baking tray with tin foil and drizzle with olive oil. Place the trout fillets on the tray and spoon the breadcrumb mixture on top.

4 Cook in the preheated oven for 17–20 minutes. You can test to see if it's cooked by inserting a knife in the centre – the flesh should be opaque. Don't overcook it, as it will become dry.

5 Serve with rice, couscous or delicious hot spuds and a dollop of butter.

Looking for a getaway weekend, with walks on the beach followed by a siesta in a four-poster bed with a blazing open fire, a view of the Atlantic and topped with an intimate dinner of delicious fish cooked impeccably? Well, I have the spot for you: **Moy House** *in Lahinch, Co. Clare is a beautiful 18th-century whitewashed house set in 15 acres of grounds overlooking Lahinch Bay. The rooms are spacious, with four-poster beds and blazing open fires. Chef Daniel O'Brien is a fabulous young budding chef with a creative mind and a careful hand with cooking. I feasted on smoked fish from the Burren Smokehouse and sweet locally dredged scallops. And you can be sure of a warm welcome from the lovely Brid O'Meara. Moy House, Lahinch, Co. Clare. Tel: +353 (0)65 708 2800* **www.moyhouse.com**

Sally's Hot Smoked Tuna Carbonara

SERVES 4

This recipe was described to me by the wonderful Sally Barnes (read more about her on p. 117) when I visited her while writing this book. Her hot smoked tuna is fantastic, and when we were leaving she gave me a piece to cook with. When we got back to our cottage in Cashelfean, I headed straight to the kitchen to cook this recipe. It can only be described as the perfect Italian/Irish marriage.

> **600g spaghetti or farfalle pasta**
> **2 eggs**
> **70g Parmesan cheese, finely grated**
> **sea salt and freshly ground black pepper**
> **olive oil**
> **150g hot smoked tuna, diced**
> **1 sprig fresh flat leaf parsley**

1 Cook the pasta in a large saucepan of boiling salted water for 10 minutes, or until the pasta is cooked.

2 While the pasta is cooking, crack the eggs into a bowl with the Parmesan cheese, salt and pepper and whisk gently.

3 Place a frying pan over a medium heat, add a tiny drop of olive oil and add in the diced hot smoked tuna. Leave to cook for just 2 minutes (this is just to warm it through, as it is already cooked).

4 Drain the spaghetti and return it to the saucepan. Pour the egg mixture into the pasta along with the hot smoked tuna and mix well, making sure the pasta is coated with the eggs. Transfer to a warm serving bowl.

5 Tear the leaves off the sprig of parsley and sprinkle over the pasta.

Tuna and Tomato Pasta from Puglia

SERVES 4

This is a fabulous store cupboard recipe that takes about 20 minutes to make – a perfect midweek supper.

> **olive oil**
> **1 garlic clove, crushed**
> **800g tinned tomatoes**
> **600g spaghetti**
> **100g tinned tuna**
> **1 tsp dried oregano**
> **sea salt and freshly ground black pepper**

1 Place a saucepan over a medium heat and add a good dollop of olive oil. Add the garlic and fry for 30 seconds. Add in the tomatoes and leave to cook for 4 minutes.

2 Meanwhile, start cooking the spaghetti in a large pan of salted boiling water.

3 Drain the tuna from the can and sprinkle over the oregano and salt and pepper. Break up the tuna with a fork.

4 Add the tuna to the tomato sauce and leave to cook for a further minute or two. Serve hot with the spaghetti.

Carpaccio of Tuna, Lemon and Sea Salt

SERVES 2

Italians eat a lot of raw fish, which I love. The fish needs to be leaping with freshness and all that is needed is a fresh lemon and some really good sea salt. Halen Môn sea salt from Wales is fantastic.

2 fresh tuna steaks
juice and zest of 1 unwaxed lemon
sea salt
good-quality extra virgin olive oil

1   Cut the tuna into slices as thin as possible and arrange on 2 plates.
2   Sprinkle sea salt over the tuna, followed with the juice and zest of a lemon and a drizzle of extra virgin olive oil. That's it!

VARIATIONS

Carpaccio of Tuna with Capers and Dill
• Scatter 6 capers over each plate.
• Sprinkle 1 tsp fresh dill over each plate.

Carpaccio of Tuna with Chilli, Fresh Ginger and Lime
• Omit the lemon and use a lime instead.
• Deseed and finely dice 1 red chilli and sprinkle over each plate.
• Grate a 1cm piece of fresh ginger over the carpaccio of tuna.

Fried Whitebait with Spicy Tomato Sauce

SERVES 2

You'll find this dish in bars and restaurants all along the Mediterranean coast. I have many memories of looking out to the Med with a glass of crisp, flowery white wine and a platter of fried whitebait and a spicy tomato sauce.

10 whitebait
1 egg, beaten
50g flour
500ml vegetable oil, for deep-frying

FOR THE SPICY TOMATO SAUCE:
2 tbsp extra virgin olive oil
$^1/_2$ onion, diced
1 garlic clove, crushed
400g tinned plum tomatoes
1 tsp paprika
sea salt and freshly ground black pepper

1 Start the tomato sauce by heating the olive oil in a saucepan over a medium heat. Add the onion and garlic, cover and leave to sweat for 2 minutes.

2 Add the tomatoes and paprika and season with salt and pepper. Cook for a further 5 minutes.

3 Meanwhile, coat the whitebait first in the beaten egg and then the flour while heating the vegetable oil for deep-frying in a wok or deep fat fryer.

4 Fry the whitebait in the hot oil until golden. Remove and drain on kitchen paper. Serve at once with the spicy tomato sauce drizzled over.

Sardines in a Blanket of Garlic and Crusty Breadcrumbs

SERVES 4

This is a great recipe that I picked up in Sicily. Crunchy, creamy and basking in flavour!

> 1kg small sardines
> sea salt and freshly ground black pepper
> 3 garlic cloves, crushed
> 2 tbsp chopped fresh parsley
> juice of 1 lemon
> 150ml white wine
> 80ml olive oil
> 3 tbsp breadcrumbs

1 Preheat the oven to 180°C.
2 Rinse the sardines and pat dry, then season with salt and pepper.
3 Brush a shallow baking dish with olive oil and lay in the sardines like soldiers, side by side.
4 Place the garlic, parsley, lemon juice, white wine and olive oil in a bowl and whisk together well.
5 Pour the liquid over the sardines, then scatter the breadcrumbs on top like a blanket.
6 Cook in the preheated oven for 20 minutes.

Trout Baked with Smoked Bacon Lardons and Baby Carrots

SERVES 2

Smoked bacon cooked with trout is a classic combination. The smoky flavours infuse into the oils of the trout and the carrots get all the joy of being drenched in the juices.

> 12 baby carrots, cleaned
> 100g smoked bacon lardons
> 1 whole trout, approx. 800g, gutted and cleaned
> sea salt and freshly ground black pepper
> olive oil
> 1 sprig fresh thyme
> creamy mustard potatoes, to serve (see p. 178)

1 Preheat the oven to 180°C.

2 Arrange the baby carrots in a line lengthways in a roasting dish.

3 Stuff half the lardons in the trout's cavity, then place the fish lengthways on top of the baby carrots.

4 Place the remaining lardons on top of the fish and season with salt and pepper.

5 Drizzle a good dollop of olive oil over the fish and add a sprig of fresh thyme to the dish.

6 Cook in the preheated oven for 20 minutes. Serve with creamy mustard potatoes (see p. 178).

Anchovy and Red Pepper Toasts

SERVES 4 AS AN APPETISER

In every tapas bar in Spain, you'll see people hunched at the bar feasting on anchovy toasts. I love them with the sweet roasted peppers, though you can replace the red peppers with some finely chopped black olives, a crumble of feta or a quail's egg.

1 red pepper	1 baguette
9 flat anchovy fillets	1 garlic clove
juice of 1 lemon	extra virgin olive oil
freshly ground black pepper	

1 Preheat the oven to 200°C.

2 First, roast the red pepper. Brush the pepper with olive oil and place in the preheated oven for 15 minutes. Then transfer to a bowl, cover with cling film and leave for 10 minutes. (Covering the bowl creates a steam that helps lift the outer skin off the pepper.)

3 After 5 minutes, take the pepper out of the bowl and remove the seeds and outer skin. Cut the roasted pepper into strips and set aside.

4 Drain, clean and pat dry the anchovy fillets, then mash them with a squeeze of lemon juice and some freshly ground black pepper.

5 Slice the baguette, rub each slice with the clove of garlic and brush with olive oil. Place on a baking tray and pop into the preheated oven for 10 minutes.

6 Remove the slices of bread from the oven and smear each one with the smooth anchovy paste, placing a strip of roasted red pepper on top.

The Fishy Fishy Café *in Kinsale, Co. Cork is probably the most famous fish restaurant in Ireland, and for good reason. Martin Healy and his team obtain and cook the best fish in the country. Sitting outside on a summer's day, you could almost imagine you're in Australia. The design of the restaurant is fantastic, with a glass wall to the kitchen so you can see the chefs in action and beautiful local art and sculptures around every corner. But the freshness of the fish makes you realise that you are in fact in one of the best fishing villages in Ireland. Make sure to pop up to their fish shop before you head home. They won't take reservations and you might have to wait, but you can sit at their bar and enjoy an aperitif in anticipation. Fishy Fishy Café, Pier Road, Kinsale, Co. Cork. Tel: +353 (0)21 470 0415* **www.fishyfishy.ie**

Bagna Càuda

Bagna càuda is a typical dish from Piedmont (northern Italy) that literally means 'hot bath'. It's one of the most popular dips in northern Italy, but you need to be prepared for the first scoop!

100g butter
100ml extra virgin olive oil
100g garlic cloves, crushed
100g salted anchovy fillets, finely chopped
2 red peppers
2 yellow peppers

1 Place a saucepan over a low heat and add the butter and olive oil.
2 Once the butter has melted, add the garlic and anchovies and simmer for 10 minutes. Remove from the saucepan and grind in a pestle and mortar.
3 Slice the peppers into boat-like strips.
4 Place the garlic and anchovy paste (it's now bagna càuda) in a bowl in the centre of a platter or plate and arrange the peppers around the plate. Scoop up the bagna càuda with the peppers and eat!

GUINNESS
Proud Sponsor
of Your Festival
SOLD HERE
GUINNESS
Proud Sponsor
of Your Festival
TRIPE SUPPERS
1/- Each

Peter and Brigitta Curtin

You can't really mention the Burren Smokehouse at Lisdoonvarna without also mentioning the Roadside Inn just 200 feet or so down the road. Both are owned and run by Brigitta and Peter Curtin and both are real focal points for the local community and visitors to the Burren area.

The Burren Smokehouse is famed for its fabulous smoked fish products such as hot honey smoked salmon, gravadlax, trout, eel, mackerel and Arctic charr. You can buy the products in the visitors' centre built above the smokehouse, along with a stunning array of local gourmet foods. The centre is well stocked with pâtés, cheese, bread, chutneys, oils and vinegar, chocolates and even wine from the Glengalliagh Valley, produced using local berries and fruits. They also sell high-quality locally produced crafts, including leatherwork, knitwear, pottery, woodwork, jewellery, CDs and books of local interest. You can listen to the music sold in the visitor centre live in the Roadside Tavern. You can also eat smoked fish platters from the smokehouse and meet many of the local producers here, dropping in for a swift half and a chat.

Brigitta and Peter are not only passionate and innovative about their own business, they are also tireless campaigners about issues affecting the local community and the Irish food industry. Recently, Brigitta has been promoting the idea of buying locally produced food as a way to keep fuel costs down. She also runs the Burren Slow Food Festival, is an active member of Good Food Ireland and runs educational workshops for both adults and kids about fish and how to smoke fish.

If ever two people were destined to meet, it is Peter and Brigitta. Brigitta was born in Sweden and grew up fishing on the Baltic Sea. Peter was born in Lisdoonvarna and grew up dredging scallops in Galway Bay. In 1981, Brigitta came to Galway looking for 'music, the Celtic spirit and the Atlantic Sea'. She walked into the Roadside Inn, the Curtin family pub, saw Peter and knew she'd found what she was looking for. At the time she was studying marine biology in Sweden but got a transfer to Galway to study algae. Peter was still working on his fishing boat and helping out in the pub.

As tourism slowed in the 1980s, Peter started looking for a new venture. He knew about baking, as the pub had always done their own, and he reckoned smoking must be fairly similar. As Peter, a big man with a big personality, tells it, 'I loved fishing, I knew about baking, tourism was crap, so I bought a kiln.' He brought the kiln over from Sweden and started smoking eel and mackerel. Initially he was smoking the fish and selling it in the pub. Then he took a shed next to the pub and expanded the business, selling to passersby and to the Gregans Castle Hotel and restaurant. Brigitta started introducing her Swedish influence with the addition of spices and herbs, such as mustard seeds, dill and paprika.

I met and chatted with Brigitta over a mixed platter of their smoked fish, which was absolutely gorgeous. She introduced the gravadlax, a Swedish method of curing fish in marinade, to the smokehouse. I asked her how she managed to juggle so much happening in her life, including being a mum to four children. She admitted that the most taxing role was being a mum and getting that balance right. She is also careful to separate her business relationship with Peter from her marriage.

It is important to Brigitta that when people come to the Burren area that they really experience it – the food, the people, the crafts and the music. That is her aim with the smokehouse and the Roadside Inn. People can call in at the visitors' centre to buy products from and learn about the area. They can drop in at the Roadside Inn and enjoy traditional Irish music, mix with the locals and eat great pub grub sourced locally.

The pub provides a real focal point for the community. As well as the smoked fish platters provided by the smokehouse, they do excellent traditional dishes like bacon and cabbage. The day I was there, an elderly widower dropped in for his bacon and cabbage with a glass of milk. Everyone in the pub said hello to him. It wasn't just a good meal for him – it was the hub of his social life. Many of the local farmers come in for their main meal of the day, to catch up on local news and to thaw out by the huge open fire. The pub has been in the Curtin family since 1893. Peter was brought up in it, so it's important to them to preserve the role of the pub as a focal point for the community.

Peter and Brigitta are a powerhouse couple who have not only built up a successful fish-smoking business, but have rooted it firmly and proudly within the context of their local community.

The Burren Smokehouse
Lisdoonvarna, Co. Clare
Tel: +353 (0)65 707 4432
E-mail: info@burrensmokehouse.ie
www.burrensmokehouse.ie

Fish al Fresco

For me, food always tastes better when eaten outdoors. Maybe it's because the fresh air creates an appetite for food, or maybe it's just the sweet joy of eating on one of our many beautiful beaches. The sun doesn't have to be splitting the stones for you to enjoy an outdoor feast – just pack a couple of rugs if there's a chill in the air. It's all about the experience of creating an occasion (although it's another story if it rains). While we were making this book, I had this longing to cook on the beaches in West Cork, so I called upon a friend, Fingal

Ferguson, who makes fabulous bacon, sausages and charcuterie at the Gubbeen Smokehouse, and we decided that if the following day was dry, we would cook a paella on the beach.

I dived out of bed the following morning in anticipation of the weather, and there to greet me was a crisp sunny winter day (yes, Ireland has lots of sunny days in November!). So Alberto and I packed up the car with rugs, a foldable table, jars of salt, pepper, spices, rice and a few saucepans. We headed down to the pier in Schull and bought some fresh fish, then went up to the smokehouse to collect Fingal with his chorizo and paella pan and headed off to the beach. Fingal built a simple but great fire by gathering large stones and building a well-like shape with them, then placing wood gathered from the beach in the well and setting it alight. Within minutes, we had a smouldering outdoor oven. The pan was placed on the fire and Fingal's delicious chorizo began to crisp, followed by the rice, stock, fresh fish and saffron. Half an hour later, I and the boys were perched on the rocks feasting on paella, the sun warming our cheeks, and wondering if we were really in Ireland.

Seafood Paella

SERVES 12

If you think of a Spanish national dish, my guess is that the first one that comes into your head is paella. A beautiful-looking, robust dish, it's served all over Spain in many different forms, but its place of origin is Valencia. The main ingredient in paella is rice, typically short-grained calasparra rice grown in the mountains of the Spanish province of Murcia. A traditional paella pan is anything from seven inches to a yard across with low sides about an inch and a half high that flare out slightly at the top and two large handles at the side. The pans don't come with a lid because paella is not cooked with a lid on. Usually made of carbon steel, they do require seasoning before cooking and will rust if they are left wet, so do wipe them with a coating of olive oil after cooking.

The authentic way to cook paella is over an open barbecue with kindling wood, but it tastes just as good cooked well in a domestic kitchen.

There are still extensive rice fields in the Valencia region, plenty of farms with plump chickens and rabbits and also rich soil perfect for growing good fresh vegetables. Consequently, the main ingredients of a typical Valencia paella are chicken, rabbit, tomatoes, green beans, saffron and sweet paprika. However, there are many varieties of paella, with prawns and shellfish added in the coastal regions – which I am partial to.

The starting point with any paella is the softened sweet onions, garlic and peppers. This is called the sofrito *– this takes a little time, but it's an important stage because if the onions aren't softened and sweet, it affects the flavour of the dish. The main difference between an Italian risotto and a Spanish paella are that a risotto is wet, while in paella, the grains of rice remain separate and each one should be coated with olive oil. The overall dish should not, however, be greasy. Also, while a risotto is constantly stirred, paella is left to cook untouched and absorb the liquid, just given a gentle shake halfway through.*

I love paella not just because of the delicious taste, but because I think it is an enormously social dish, shared by families and often served at falles (local fairs) and at big picnics. In Spain, there are competitions to cook the largest paellas – I believe the biggest one was cooked in Valencia. It measured 20 metres in diameter and was eaten by 100,000 people. You can't get more convivial than that!

olive oil
20cm piece of Gubbeen chorizo, sliced
2 onions, diced
4 garlic cloves, crushed
500g paella rice
sea salt and freshly ground black pepper
1 tsp paprika
1l fish stock, kept hot
pinch of saffron
500g monkfish
1kg mussels, cleaned and de-bearded
10 prawns, left whole, raw and unshelled
6 red piquillo peppers
2 lemons, cut into wedges to serve

1   Heat a large paella pan over a medium heat. Add a drop of olive oil followed by
    the chorizo. Leave to crisp for about 5 minutes, then add the onions and garlic
    and cook for a further 10 minutes.

2   Stir in the rice and season with salt and pepper. Add the paprika, hot fish stock
    and saffron and leave to simmer for about 15 minutes.

3   Scatter the pieces of monkfish over the rice and push under the surface with the
    back of a spoon. Lay the mussels and prawns over the top and simmer for
    another 10 minutes, until the mussels have opened and the prawns are pink.
    After 5 minutes, lay the red piquillo peppers on top, to warm through. Serve with
    lemon wedges around the pan.

TIPS:
  ▪ You can add mussels, shrimps, hake – practically any kind of fish – to this dish
  ▪ If you can't get your hands on piquillo peppers, then just slice up red peppers
    and add when you're cooking the onions.

What to pack for cooking on the beach

- Rug
- Foldable table
- Saucepan or griddle/frying pan (depending on what you're cooking)
- Utensils for cooking (wooden spoon, good sharp knife, spatula)
- Chopping board
- Plates
- Cutlery
- Glasses
- Napkins
- Rubbish bag (we need to keep our beaches clean!)
- Matches
- Ingredients (I suggest that you prep as much as you can at home and then transport them in plastic containers)
- Barbecue – charcoal BBQs are also great for the beach

Barbecuing

Barbecuing has taken off in Ireland big time: over 60 per cent of households now own one. And there's a dizzying variety to choose from: gas burners, charcoal burners, optional hoods, self-cleaning grills, added griddles, warming racks and even wheels for easy manoeuvrability. There is also a bewildering choice of barbecue fuel to choose from.

The most popular barbecue fuel is briquettes. The problem with charcoal briquettes is that they release 105 times more carbon monoxide per unit of energy than propane. Propane is a by-product of petroleum and it may burn more cleanly than briquettes, but it's still a fossil fuel and a contributor to global atmospheric CO_2 levels. So what's the answer? Charcoal is carbon neutral, but even then, 90 per cent of the charcoal we burn is sourced from unsustainable tropical rainforests. The best option is to buy from charcoal producers who practise the art of coppicing. Coppicers cut stems from trees on a 10 to 15-year cycle and also use thinnings and waste wood from mature fallen trees. The charcoal is created by carbonising the wood as it smoulders under turf or in specially built kilns.

So you have your barbecue and your sustainable fuel – now all you have to worry about is your repertoire. Pat a wet, raw salmon with a mix of spices and grill at a high temperature until the spices form a crisp coating on the outside, while the salmon cooks gently inside. It tastes great and because it's cooked outside on the barbecue, the house isn't left smelling of fish for the next week. Courgettes, aubergines, squash, tomatoes, onions and mushrooms are great barbecued on their own or skewered in a kebab with peppers and tofu or halloumi cheese. Nectarines, peaches, bananas and mango make fantastic desserts, marinated in brandy and honey with a spice of your choice, then barbecued and served with a dollop of crème fraîche.

Sauces and marinades work well with barbecued food. Broadly speaking, sauces are vinegar based and are basted onto the fish, whereas marinades are used to soak the fish before cooking.

One of the best things about barbecues is the social aspect – family and friends enjoying food and a drink, kids tumbling around and everyone contributing something to the meal. Some of the best salads I have ever eaten have been brought along by friends to barbecues, so for all you grill jockeys out there, here is your chance to have a go. Expand your repertoire and try some of these amazing marinades, served with a stunning salad. What more could you want except great company, good weather and an understanding neighbour?

Tips for the barbecue or hand-built fire on the beach

- If you have any rosemary or thyme growing in the garden, cut off some sprigs and throw them on the fire right before you start to cook. As they burn, they release fantastic flavours into the food.
- Only start cooking over the fire/BBQ when the fire and smoke have died down and you have very hot red embers.
- Have a long tongs (so you don't burn yourself) and a brush (to clean the grill).
- Have a little table beside the fire/BBQ for all your oils, seasonings, marinades, etc.

Marinades for Fish

Spicy Marinade

This is great on all fish.

150ml olive oil
1 onion, finely diced
juice of 1 lemon
3 garlic cloves, crushed
3 tsp ground cumin
2 tsp paprika
$^1/_2$ tsp turmeric

Zesty Marinade

Perfect for oily fish such as mackerel, trout or herring.

juice of 2 limes
2 garlic cloves, crushed
1 tbsp ground cumin
1 tbsp ground coriander
3 tbsp finely chopped fresh coriander
sea salt and freshly ground black pepper

Indian Marinade

Great for meaty fish like hake or haddock.

$^1/_2$ cup yoghurt
2 tbsp sunflower oil
1 tbsp ground cumin
1 tsp ground turmeric
$^1/_2$ tsp ground coriander
1 tbsp finely chopped fresh coriander

Japanese Marinade

This delicate marinade works well on flat and oily fish.

$^1/_2$ **cup sunflower oil**
$^1/_4$ **cup rice wine vinegar**
3 tbsp soy sauce
3 tbsp chopped fresh ginger
2 tbsp sugar

1   Place all the ingredients in a bowl and mix well.
2   Pour the marinade over the fish and leave to marinate in a fridge for 2 hours.
3   Depending on the size of the fillet of fish, cook for approximately 3–5 minutes on each side.

TIP: Have a look at pp. 182–6 for suggestions on salads.

Great Sauces for Fish

The word 'sauce' is a French word that means a relish to make food more appetizing. When you first learn to cook, you're taught the basics like soup and bread. Then you go on to learn the 'master sauces', which are also known as the 'mother sauces'. They are the classic sauces that you will use over and over again when cooking and are fantastic to have in your repertoire because you can go on to add in so many different variations and the task of cooking becomes so much more enjoyable and easy. As well as the classic sauces, I've also included salsas and pesto. All are delicious blanketed over a poached, grilled or roasted fish or alongside some fried seafood.

Herb Butter

MAKES APPROX. 100g

> 1 tbsp fresh herbs (basil, thyme, coriander, rosemary, dill or fennel)
> 100g butter, softened

1 Finely chop the herbs and place them in a mixing bowl. Add the softened butter to the bowl. Beat well, until all the herbs are well mixed through the butter.
2 Tip the butter out onto a piece of cling film and shape the butter into a log about 2 ½cm in diameter.
3 Wrap the log in the cling film and place in the fridge to set, about 1 hour.

VARIATIONS

Chilli and Coriander Butter

• Use 1 tsp finely chopped chilli and 1 tbsp fresh coriander.

Orange and Hazelnut Butter

• Beat in the juice and zest of half an orange with the butter.
• Replace the herbs with 1 tbsp roasted, finely chopped hazelnuts.

Pine Nut and Basil Butter

• Mix 1 tbsp fresh basil into the butter.
• Beat 2 tbsp finely chopped pine nuts into the butter.

Red Pepper Salsa

SERVES 2

> 1 red pepper, diced
> 1 small red chilli, diced
> juice of 2 limes
> 1 garlic clove, crushed
> ½ tsp honey
> sea salt and freshly ground black pepper

1 Place all the ingredients in a bowl. Season to taste and mix well.

Mornay Sauce

SERVES 4

30g butter
30g plain flour
620ml milk
sea salt and freshly ground black pepper

1   Place a saucepan over a medium heat and melt the butter. Once the butter has melted, whisk in the flour until you get a thick paste.
2   Gradually whisk in the milk until you reach a smooth consistency.
3   Lower the heat and allow to simmer for 5 minutes. Season to taste.

VARIATIONS

Cheese Sauce
• Whisk in 100g of good-quality Cheddar or Gouda to the sauce after the milk to make a delicious cheese sauce.

Hollandaise Sauce

SERVES 4

3 egg yolks
150g butter, cubed
1 dessertspoon white wine vinegar or juice of 1 lemon
salt and freshly ground white pepper

1   Place a small saucepan over a low heat and pour in the egg yolks. Add the cubes of butter one at a time and whisk into the eggs. Once all the butter has been melted, the sauce should begin to thicken.
2   Remove from the heat and stir in the white wine vinegar or the juice of one freshly squeezed lemon. Season to taste.

VARIATIONS

Creamy Spinach Sauce
• Blanch a fistful of fresh spinach in boiling water, drain, chop up and stir into the hollandaise sauce.

Béarnaise Sauce
• Sweat together 50ml white vinegar, 1 diced shallot and 1 tsp tarragon. Allow to reduce.
• Sieve, then add to the hollandaise sauce.

Homemade Mayonnaise

MAKES APPROX. 200ml

3 eggs yolks
1 tsp Dijon mustard
pinch salt
1 tablespoon white wine vinegar
100ml extra virgin olive oil
100ml vegetable oil

1 In a bowl, crack in 3 egg yolks, followed by the Dijon mustard, a pinch of salt and the white wine vinegar.

2 Measure out 100ml of vegetable oil and 100ml of extra virgin olive oil and slowly whisk into the egg yolks. The mayonnaise will begin to thicken very fast.

VARIATIONS

Tartare Sauce

• Mix in 1 tsp each of finely chopped gherkins, chives, parsley and capers to the mayonnaise (see p. 56).

Herb Mayonnaise

• Mix in 1 tbsp basil, dill or coriander to the mayonnaise.

Lemon Mayonnaise

• Replace the vinegar with 2 tbsp lemon juice.

Pink Mayonnaise

• Mix 1 tbsp tomato purée into the mayonnaise.

Basil Pesto

MAKES APPROX. 200ml

    110g fresh basil leaves
    150ml extra virgin olive oil
    1 garlic clove
    30g pine nuts
    50g freshly grated Parmesan (I use Parmigiano Reggiano)
    pinch salt

Put all the ingredients into a food processor and blend.

VARIATIONS

Coriander, Parsley, Watercress or Rocket Pesto

• Substitute coriander, parsley, watercress or rocket for the basil.

Creamy Hazelnut Pesto

• Replace the pine nuts with hazelnuts.

• Add in 50g soft goat's cheese.

Spicy Tomato Salsa

SERVES 4

    olive oil
    1 red chilli, deseeded
    1 garlic clove, crushed
    1 red pepper, quartered and deseeded
    4 ripe plum tomatoes, diced
    50g toasted almonds
    salt and freshly ground black pepper
    fresh basil or coriander (optional)

1 Place a small saucepan over a medium heat and add a dollop of olive oil.
2 Add the chilli, crushed garlic and red pepper to the pan and leave to simmer for 2 minutes.
3 Add the diced tomatoes and toasted almonds. Season with salt and pepper, lower the heat and allow to simmer for 10 minutes.
4 Add fresh basil or coriander at the end if you wish.

Salsa Verde

MAKES APPROX. 120ml
>   4 fresh basil sprigs
>   1 tbsp white wine vinegar
>   1 sprig parsley
>   2 garlic cloves, crushed
>   2 anchovy fillets, chopped
>   2 tbsp capers
>   100ml extra virgin olive oil

1   Take the basil leaves off the stem and place in a food processor.
2   Add the rest of the ingredients and blend until the mixture reaches a smooth consistency.

Alongside
the Fish

Potato Roasties

SERVES 4

500g potatoes, peeled and chopped into small cubes
80ml olive oil
50g butter
1 garlic clove, left whole
1 sprig rosemary
sea salt and freshly ground black pepper

1 Preheat the oven to 200°C.
2 Place the potatoes in a saucepan of boiling salted water for 5 minutes, then drain and transfer to a roasting dish.
3 Drizzle the olive oil over the potatoes, then place the butter, garlic clove and sprig of rosemary on top of the potatoes. Season with salt and pepper.
4 Cook in the preheated oven for 10 minutes, or until golden and cooked all the way through.

Wet Polenta

SERVES 6

1.5 litres water
sea salt
350g polenta flour (not the instant kind, the flour)
extra virgin olive oil

1 Bring the water to the boil in a large saucepan and add a good pinch of salt.
2 Slowly add the polenta, whisking quickly. Be careful to not leave any lumps.
3 Reduce the heat to low and cook for a further 40 minutes, stirring every 10 minutes. Stir in a good dollop of extra virgin olive oil just before serving.

Note: The relation between flour and water varies according to the type of flour, so be ready to add some boiling water or polenta flour if the mixture looks too thick or runny.

Creamy Gratin Dauphinois

SERVES 4

> butter, for greasing
> 1 garlic clove, crushed
> 6 potatoes, thinly sliced
> 1 pint creamy milk (half cream/milk)
> sea salt and freshly ground black pepper

1 Preheat the oven to 170°C and set a pot of water on to boil.

2 Grease a 15cm x 15cm roasting dish with butter and sprinkle the crushed garlic on the bottom of the dish.

3 Drop the sliced potatoes into the pot of boiling water and boil for 4–5 minutes, then drain.

4 Make layers of potatoes in the dish, seasoning each layer. Pour the creamy milk over the potatoes, pushing the potatoes down until they are completely immersed in the creamy milk. Cover with a butter wrapper.

3 Cook in the preheated oven for 30 minutes, then remove the butter wrapper and turn up the heat to 200°C and cook for another 10 minutes, until the top is golden.

Creamy Mustard Potatoes

SERVES 4

> 400g potatoes, peeled
> 50g butter
> 1 tbsp English mustard powder
> 1 tbsp yellow mustard seeds
> 100ml warm milk
> salt and pepper, to taste

1 Boil or steam the potatoes until tender. Drain.

2 Using a potato masher, mash the potatoes while hot in the pan, adding the butter, mustard powder and seeds, and a pinch of salt and pepper.

3 Loosen the texture with warm milk and transfer to a warmed dish.

Ratatouille

SERVES 6

1 aubergine
1 courgette
1 red pepper
1 yellow pepper
1 garlic clove
1 x 400g tin plum tomatoes
sea salt and freshly ground black pepper
olive oil
bunch of fresh basil, leaves only

1 Preheat the oven to 170°C.

2 Slice the aubergine, courgette and peppers into wedges.

3 Place the vegetables, garlic and tomatoes in a roasting dish. Season with salt and pepper, add a dollop of olive oil and mix well.

4 Cook in the preheated oven for 30 minutes, or until the vegetables are tender. Stir in the fresh basil leaves just before serving.

TIP:

- If you don't have any fresh basil, you could sprinkle 1 tsp of dried herbs into the roasting dish before you put it in the oven.
- This is great served as a side dish with roasted fish.

Honey-roasted Butternut Squash with Rosemary

SERVES 4

600g butternut squash or turnip
olive oil
2 tbsp clear honey
1 sprig fresh rosemary
sea salt and freshly ground black pepper

1 Preheat the oven to 180°C.
2 Peel and chop the butternut squash into small chunks. Place on a roasting tray and drizzle with olive oil and honey. Add the sprig of rosemary and season well with salt and pepper.
3 Place in the preheated oven for 30–40 minutes. After 15 minutes, take them out and give them a good toss just to make sure that they are well coated with the honey. Test to see if they are cooked at 30 minutes.

Green Beans with Tomatoes and Pine Nuts

SERVES 8

> 600g green beans (French beans)
> 70g pine nuts
> 1 x 400g tin good-quality chopped tomatoes
> sea salt and freshly ground black pepper

1   Cook the green beans in a saucepan of boiling water for 5 minutes. Drain and set aside.
2   Place the pine nuts in the saucepan and lightly toast on a medium heat.
3   Once they begin to colour, add in the tomatoes, season with salt and pepper and allow to cook for 3–4 minutes.
4   Stir in the green beans and cook for 2 minutes. Serve straight away.

TIP: This dish is also delicious cold as a salad – just add a drizzle of good extra virgin olive oil.

Creamy Lemon Potato Salad

SERVES 6

> 1kg new potatoes, washed
> 300ml crème fraîche
> zest and juice of 2 lemons
> sea salt and freshly ground black pepper
> 1 bunch fresh mint, chopped

1   Boil the potatoes in a small amount of salted water (almost steaming them) until tender, then drain and allow to cool enough to handle them. Cut the potatoes into quarters and place them in a large bowl.
2   While the potatoes are still warm, pour in the crème fraîche, lemon juice and zest and season with salt and pepper. Leave to cool. Mix in the fresh mint just before serving.

Summer Couscous Salad

SERVES 6

250g couscous
500ml vegetable stock, boiling
70g flaked almonds (or pine nuts or hazelnuts), toasted
100g dried apricots, roughly chopped
bunch of fresh rocket
sea salt and freshly ground black pepper
extra virgin olive oil

1 Place the couscous in a large bowl and pour over the boiling vegetable stock. Cover with cling film and leave to steam for about 10 minutes, then fluff up the couscous with a fork.

2 Mix the toasted flaked almonds, apricots and rocket in a large bowl.

3 Add the couscous to the large bowl with the almonds, apricots and rocket and mix together well. Season with salt and pepper and a stir in a good dollop of the extra virgin olive oil.

TIPS

- You can substitute fresh coriander for the rocket.
- Instead of the apricots, you can use raisins or sun-dried tomatoes.
- Crumbled feta cheese is also delicious folded through the salad.

Spinach, Chickpea, Lemon and Soft Goat's Cheese Salad

SERVES 2

bunch of fresh baby spinach leaves, washed
100g cooked chickpeas
handful of hazelnuts, chopped
80g soft goat's cheese
zest of 1 unwaxed lemon
extra virgin olive oil
sea salt and freshly ground black pepper

1 Arrange the fresh baby spinach on 2 plates.

2 Sprinkle the chickpeas over the leaves, followed by the hazelnuts.

3 Crumble the soft goat's cheese over the salad, then sprinkle the lemon zest on top.

4 Finish with a drizzle of olive oil and season with sea salt and freshly ground pepper.

Greek Salad

SERVES 4

50g black Kalamata olives
3 medium tomatoes, cut into small wedges
1 cucumber, peeled and cut into small wedges
1 onion, sliced finely
100ml extra virgin olive oil
150g feta cheese
1 tbsp dried oregano
sea salt and freshly ground black pepper

Mix all the ingredients in a bowl and toss.

Lemon, Courgette and Pea Salad

SERVES 4

1 tsp sesame seeds
zest and juice of 1 lemon
100ml extra virgin olive oil
sea salt and freshly ground black pepper
400g courgettes
200g green peas

1 Place the sesame seeds, lemon juice and zest and extra virgin olive oil in a small bowl. Season with salt and pepper.
2 Thinly slice the courgettes lengthways (using a mandolin if you have one) and place in a large serving bowl or platter.
3 Place the peas in a saucepan of salted boiling water and allow to cook for 3 minutes. Drain and run under cold water. Once drained, add them to the courgettes.
4 Sprinkle the lemon dressing over the vegetables and toss.

Dressings for Green Salads

Honey and Mustard Salad Dressing

1 tsp wholegrain mustard
1 tsp honey
2 tbsp balsamic vinegar
6 tbsp extra virgin olive oil
sea salt and freshly ground black pepper

Place all the ingredients in a bowl and whisk together. Season with salt and pepper to taste.

Thyme and Garlic Dressing

1 tbsp white wine vinegar
1 tbsp lemon juice
1 tsp fresh thyme leaves
1 garlic clove, crushed
1 tsp Dijon mustard,
6 tbsp extra virgin olive oil
sea salt and ground black pepper

Place all the ingredients in a bowl and whisk together. Season with salt and pepper to taste.

After the Fish

Honey-roasted Peaches

SERVES 4

> **8 peaches**
> **40g butter**
> **honey**
> **vanilla ice cream, to serve**

1 Preheat the oven to 200°C.
2 Cut the peaches in half, remove the stones and place the halved peaches in a roasting dish or baking tray.
2 Put a small knob of butter in the 'nest' (where you removed the stone) of each peach and drizzle the honey over.
3 Cook in the preheated oven for 15 minutes. Delicious served warm or cold with vanilla ice cream.

Raspberry and Lemon Granita

SERVES 4

> **50ml water**
> **200g caster sugar**
> **550g raspberries**
> **juice and zest of 1 lemon**

1 Make a sugar syrup by placing the water and 150g of the caster sugar into a saucepan. Gently heat until the sugar has completely dissolved and allow to cool.
2 Crush the raspberries and mix together with the remaining sugar and lemon juice and zest.
3 Churn in an ice-cream maker or freeze in a shallow container, stirring every half an hour until set.

Pistachio Chocolate Pots

SERVES 4

150g dark chocolate
80ml cream
2 tbsp finely chopped pistachios
3 eggs, separated

1 Break the chocolate into small pieces and place in a glass or Pyrex bowl suspended over a saucepan of simmering water.

2 Stir the chocolate with a wooden spoon until it has melted into a silky smooth thick liquid.

3 Remove the bowl from the saucepan and stir in the cream and pistachios.

4 Break the egg whites into a separate bowl and add the yolks into the chocolate mixture. Mix the yolks into the chocolate.

5 Beat the egg whites until you get a stiff peak, then gently fold the stiff egg whites into the chocolate mixture.

6 Pour the chocolate mousse into a large serving bowl or individual small glasses.

7 Place in a fridge to chill for 1 hour to allow the mousse to set.

VARIATIONS

- Just before adding in the egg whites, you can stir in fresh raspberries, blackberries, strawberries (chopped) or chopped hazelnuts, almonds or pine nuts.

- A fun way of serving this chocolate mousse is to pour the mixture into espresso cups, allow it to set and serve with amaretti biscuits.

- A tablespoon of cognac or rum is also beautiful with the mousse. Add this in with the egg yolks.

- For an orange chocolate mousse, stir in the juice of 1 and the zest of half an orange with the cream.

Summer Berry Pudding

SERVES 4

450g summer berries (raspberries, strawberries, tayberries, blackberries, redcurrants, blueberries)
130g caster sugar
juice of 1 orange
9 slices of good-quality white bread
vanilla ice cream, to serve

1   Place the berries in a saucepan and add the caster sugar and orange juice. Bring to the boil, cover and simmer for 4 minutes.

2   Sieve the mixture, separating the juice and the fruit.

3   Cut the slices of bread into thick strips and dip into the berry juice. Line a bowl with the juice-soaked bread.

4   Fill the bread-lined bowl with the fruit and cover with all the remaining juiced bread.

5   Cover with cling film and press with a weight (I usually use a saucer with a bag of rice on top). Refrigerate for 24 hours.

6   Heat the remaining juice in a pan and reduce by half to make a syrup. Cool and chill.

7   Turn out the summer pudding onto a serving plate and pour over the syrup.

8   Serve with a bowl of vanilla ice cream – summer heaven!

Strawberry Fool

SERVES 4

250–300ml cream
250g strawberries (retain one to chop up for decoration), hulled
pinch of sugar

1 Whip the cream.

2 Place the strawberries and sugar in a bowl and mash well.

3 Fold the cream into the strawberries.

TIPS:

- You can substitute other fruits if you want (or need) to – cooked rhubarb, raspberries or cooked blackcurrants are all tasty alternatives.
- Fold in roughly crushed meringues, which makes what is known as an 'Eton mess'.
- Serve in a tall glass standing on a saucer with amaretti biscuits to dip in – heaven!

Baked Lemon Ricotta Cake

SERVES 6–8

10 eggs
225g caster sugar
1.5kg ricotta cheese
1 tsp vanilla extract
juice of 1 lemon
zest of 3 lemons

1 Preheat the oven to 160°C.

2 In a mixing bowl, beat the eggs and sugar until pale yellow.

3 In another bowl, beat the ricotta until smooth.

4 Gradually add the eggs and sugar to the ricotta.

5 Stir in the vanilla extract, followed by the lemon juice and zest.

6 Pour into a 25cm springform tin and bake in the preheated oven for 75 minutes. Once cooked, the middle should be pale and the edges raised and golden brown. Remove from the tin and cool completely on a cooling rack.

7 Once cooled, remove to a plate, wrap in paper towels and place in the fridge (this will help remove the moisture). Change the paper towels once they are wet. You should leave the cake in the fridge for about 12 hours – it's worth the wait!

8 Once you have removed the cake from the fridge, allow it rest for 1 hour or so to get back up to room temperature.

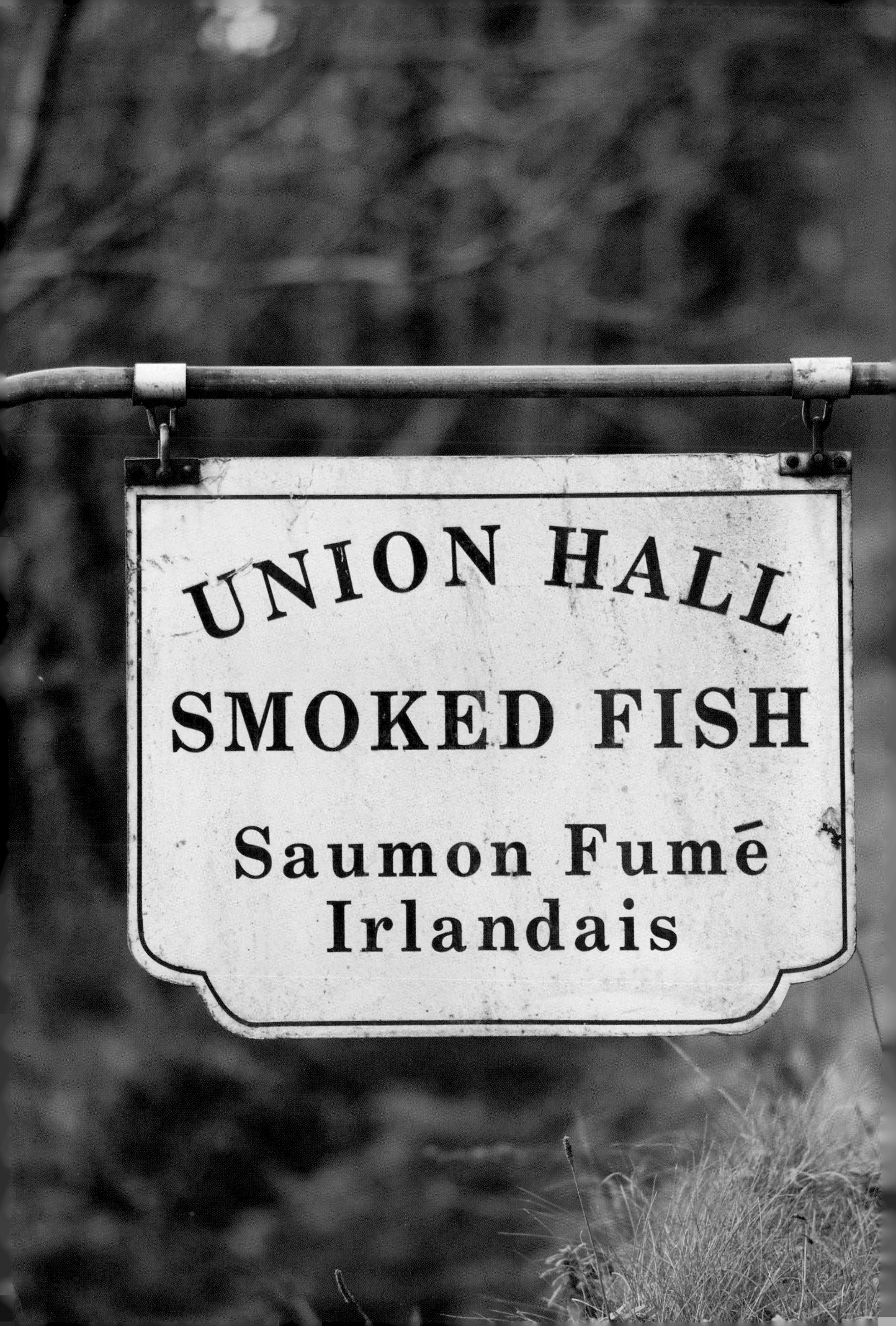
UNION HALL
SMOKED FISH
Saumon Fumé
Irlandais

Fishmongers, Shops, Market Stallholders and Buying Fish Direct

CLARE

- Burren Smokehouse, **Kincora Road, Lisdoonvarna. Tel: 065 7074432; www.burrensmokehouse.ie**

- Rene Cusack, **The Market, Ennis. Tel: 065 6892712**

CORK

- Ballycotton Seafood, **Main Street, Midleton and The English Market, Grand Parade, Cork City. Tel: 021 4646522; www.ballycottonseafood.ie**

- Belvelly Smokehouse, **Belvelly, Cobh. Tel: 021 4811089**

- Casey Fish Products, **Shanagarry, Midleton. Tel: 021 4646955**

- Central Fish Market, **New Street, Bantry. Tel: 027 53714**

- Dennehy's Fish Shop, **96 Great William O'Brien Street, Blackpool. Tel: 021 4302144**

- The Fish Shop, **Main Street, Union Hall, Cork City. Tel: 028 33818**

- Fishy Fishy Shop, **Guardwell, Kinsale. Tel: 021 4774453**

- Good Fish Processing Carrigaline Ltd, **Carrigaline Industrial Park, Carrigaline. Tel: 021 4373917**

- Kay O'Connell, **13–20 Grand Parade Market, Grand Parade, Cork City. Tel: 021 4276380; www.koconnellsfish.com**

- Normandy Ireland Ltd, **The Pier, Schull. Tel: 028 28599**

- Sean and Ollie O'Driscoll **at the following markets:**
  Midleton, Sat 8.30 a.m. – 1 p.m.
  Mahon Point, Thurs 8.30 a.m. – 2 p.m.
  Bantry, Fri 8.30 a.m. – 3 p.m.

- Ummera Smokehouse, **Inchybridge, Timoleague. Tel: 023 46644; www.ummera.com**

- Wille Martin, **The English Market, 13-20 Grand Parade, Cork City.**

DONEGAL

- O'Reilly's Fish Centre, **23 Castle Street, Ballyshannon. Tel: 071 9851389**

DUBLIN

- Beshoffs of Howth, **17–18 West Pier, Howth. Tel: 01 8390766; www.beshoffs.ie**

- Cavistons Food Emporium, **58–59 Glasthule Road, Glasthule. Tel: 01 2809120; www.cavistons.com**

- Dorans on the Pier, **7 West Pier, Howth. Tel: 01 8392419**

- J.L. Fitzsimon's Fresh Fish Shop, **183A Kimmage Road West, Crumlin Cross. Tel: 01 4554832**

- The Ice Plant, **Dun Laoghaire Pier. Tel: 01 280 5936**

- Kish Fish, **40–42 Bow Street, Smithfield. Tel: 01 8728211; www.kishfish.ie**

- Nicky's Plaice, Store F, West Pier, Howth. Tel: 01 8323557

- Smithfield Fish Market, Michan Street.

- Stevie Connolly Seafoods, Finglas Village. Tel: 086 3871160

- Thomas Molloy, 12 Lower Baggot Street.

- Wright's of Marino, 21 Marino Mart. Tel: 01 8333636; www.wrightsofmarino.com

GALWAY

- The Connemara Smokehouse, Bunowen Pier, Ballyconneely, Clifden. Tel: 095 23739; www.smokehouse.ie

- Kinvara Smokehouse, Kinvara. Tel: 091 637489; www.kinvarasmokedsalmon.com

- Seafood Centre, Galway Bay Seafoods Ltd, New Docks. Tel: 091 563011; www.galwaybayseafoods.com

KERRY

- Dingle Bay Shellfish, Ballinaboula, Dingle. Tel: 066 915 1933

- On The Wild Side, Kilcummin, Castlegregory. Tel: 066 713 9028

- Quinlan's Kerry Fish, Main Street, Cahirciveen. Tel: 066 9472686; and also The Square, Killorglin. Tel: 066 9761860; www.kerryfish.com

LIMERICK

- John Sadlier, Roches Street, Limerick City. Tel: 061 414232

- Rene Cusack, St Alphonsus Street. Tel: 061 440054

- Sean and Ollie O'Driscoll at the Limerick Market, Sat 8.30 a.m. – 2 p.m.

LOUTH

- Atlantic Catch Seafoods, 1A Stockwell Street, Drogheda. Tel: 041 9803492

- Johnny Morgan's Fish Shop, 7 Eimer Court, Market Square, Dundalk. Tel: 042 9327977

- Kirwan's Fish Cart, 55 St Laurence Street, Drogheda. Tel: 041 9830622

- Morgan Ocean Fresh Seafood, Ardaghy, Omeath. Tel: 042 9375128; www.morgansoceanfresh.ie

MAYO

- Clarke's Seafood Delicatessen, O'Rahilly Street, Ballina. Tel: 096 21022; also Peter Street, Westport. Tel: 098 24379; www.clarkes.ie

MEATH

- Connolly Seafood, 43 Trimgate Street, Navan. Tel: 046 9072233

- Nick's Fish, Unit 9, Town Centre, Ashbourne. Tel: 01 8353555; www.nicksfish.ie

SLIGO

- Cool Springs Arctic Charr, Ballyglass, Cloonacool. Tel: 071 9184393

WESTMEATH

- Rene Cusack, Unit 8, Belhavel, Athlone. Tel: 0906 420355

WICKLOW

- Fish Out Of Water, Beech Grove, Ferrybank, Arklow. Tel: 0402 29315; www.fishoutofwater.ie

- Hooked on Fish, 8 Main Street, Wicklow Town. Tel: 0404 20747

- Moran's Seafood Specialist, La Touche Place, Greystones. Tel: 01 2876327

NORTHERN IRELAND
ANTRIM

- Morton's, 30 North Street, Ballycastle. Tel: 028 2076 2348

BANGOR

- McKeown's, 14 High Street, Bangor. Tel: 028 9127 1141

BELFAST

- Walter Ewing, 124 Shankill Road. Tel: 028 9038 1120

Supervalus nationwide stock a great selection of locally caught fish. For stocklists log on to www.supervalue.ie

Index